JOHN BYRNE

Writer ▪ Artist ▪ Letterer

TRISH MULVIHILL

Colorist

Superman created by Jerry Siegel and Joe Shuster

Batman created by Bob Kane

Jenette Kahn President & Editor-in-Chief Paul Levitz Executive Vice President & Publisher
Mike Carlin Executive Editor Joey Cavalieri Editor-original series
Dale Crain Editor-collected edition Maureen McTigue Assistant Editor-original series
Michael Wright Assistant Editor-collected edition Georg Brewer Design Director
Robbin Brosterman Art Director Richard Bruning VP-Creative Director
Patrick Caldon VP-Finance & Operations Dorothy Crouch VP-Licensed Publishing
Terri Cunningham VP-Managing Editor Joel Ehrlich Senior VP-Advertising & Promotions
Alison Gill Exec. Director-Manufacturing Lillian Laserson VP & General Counsel
Jim Lee Editorial Director-WildStorm John Nee VP & General Manager-WildStorm
Bob Wayne VP-Direct Sales

SUPERMAN & BATMAN: GENERATIONS

DC Comics, 1700 Broadway, New York, NY 10019
A division of Warner Bros. - A Time Warner Entertainment Company
Printed in Canada. First Printing. ISBN: 1-56389-605-2
Cover illustration by John Byrne. Cover color by Trish Mulvihill.

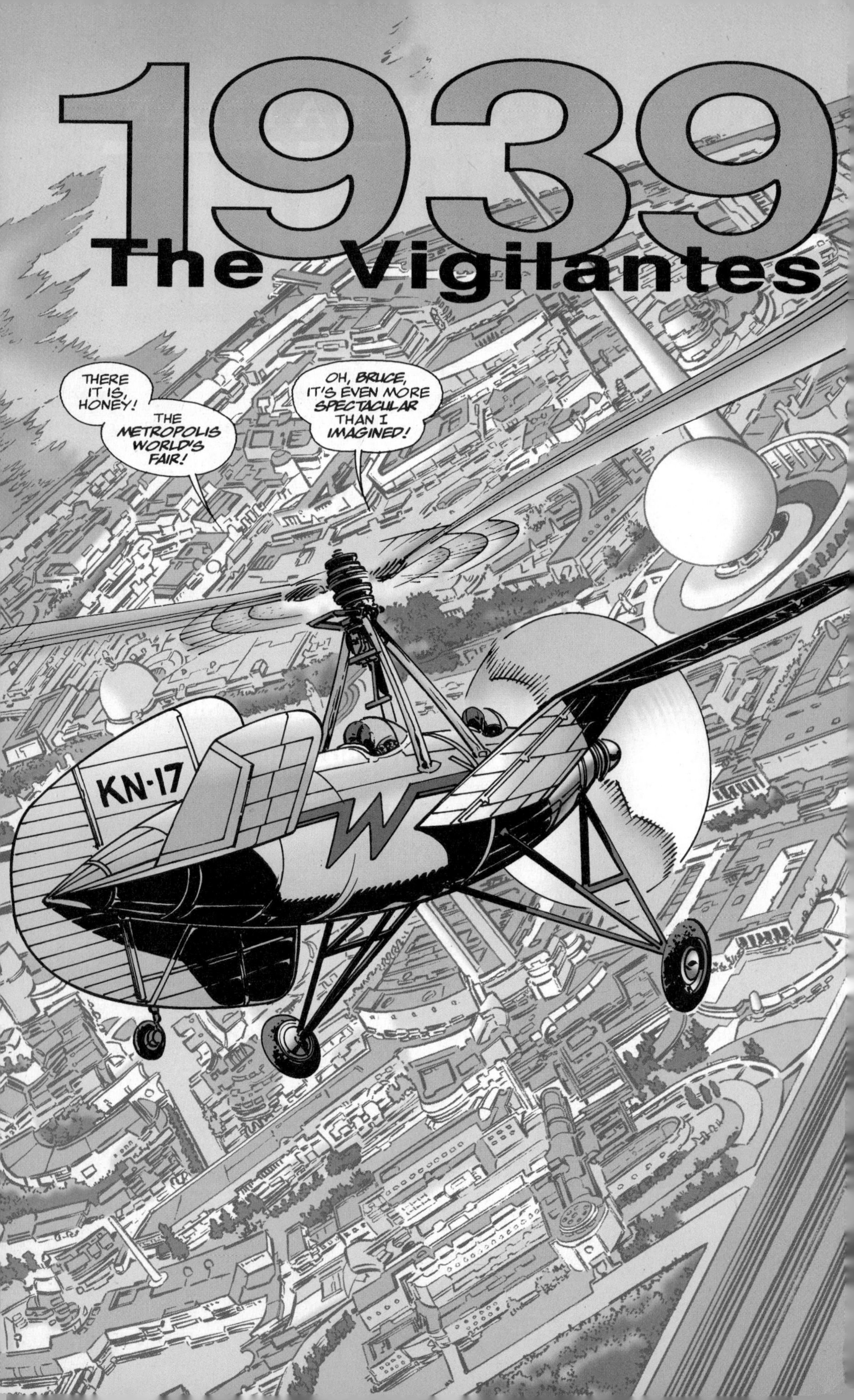
1939
The Vigilantes
THERE IT IS, HONEY!
THE METROPOLIS WORLD'S FAIR!
OH, BRUCE, IT'S EVEN MORE SPECTACULAR THAN I IMAGINED!
KN-17

BUT--I DON'T SEE ANYTHING LIKE AN AIRFIELD. WHERE ARE YOU GOING TO LAND?
ANYWHERE I WANT, JULIE! NOT MUCH POINT IN BEING THE NATION'S SEVENTH RICHEST MAN IF I CAN'T DO WHAT I PLEASE!
LOOK OUT! THAT LUNA-TIC IS GONNA LAND RIGHT ON TOP OF US!
NO CHANCE OF THAT, FRIEND. I WOULDN'T EVEN ATTEMPT THIS STUNT IF I DIDN'T THINK I COULD PLANT THIS BIRD EXACT-LY WHERE I WANT HER!
I ONLY PLAY AT BEING A BORED AND INDIFFERENT PLAYBOY--AND ONE DAY I WILL TAKE GREAT DELIGHT IN REVEALING THAT TO MY FIANCÉE!
OUT YOU COME, DARLING!
LOOKS LIKE THE WHOLE FAIR IS IN EASY WALKING DISTANCE FROM HERE!
THAT WAS RECKLESS AND UNNECESSARY, BRUCE.
YOU SHOULD KNOW BY NOW YOU DON'T HAVE TO DO THAT SORT OF THING TO IMPRESS ME!
HEY! WHAT THE HECK DO YOU THINK YOU'RE DOING?
AH, THE ANTICIPATED REPRESENTATIVES OF THE METROPOLITAN POLICE FORCE.
I'M BRUCE WAYNE, OFFICERS, AND I'M SURE WE CAN DEAL WITH THIS MATTER WITHOUT UNDUE FUSS.
BRUCE WAYNE? THE GOTHAM MILLIONAIRE?
PUT YOUR WALLET AWAY, WAYNE. YOU MAY BE ABLE TO BUY YOUR WAY OUT OF TROUBLE IN GOTHAM, BUT HERE IN METROPOLIS...
EEEEEEEEE

HOLY..!! IT'S ELECTROX !
BUT I DIDN'T THINK HE COULD MOVE AROUND LIKE THAT!!
THAT ONE GUY DOESN'T SEEM TO WANT TO GIVE GROUND, BOSS.
NOW YOU WILL ALL LEARN NOTHING THAT THE ULTRA-HUMANITE SAYS IS TO BE TAKEN LIGHTLY.
BUT I WARNED METROPOLIS THE CITY WOULD PAY DEARLY IF I DID NOT RECEIVE ONE MILLION DOLLARS BEFORE NOON TODAY.
I'M SURE YOU DIDN'T, FOOL.
BLAST! I'M SURE AS THE BAT-MAN I COULD HANDLE THIS MEN-ACE EASILY...
...BUT MY EFFEC-TIVENESS IN THAT ROLE DEPENDS ON KEEPING MY DUAL IDENTITY SECRET!
BRUCE! RUN! THAT THING WILL TRAMPLE YOU LIKE YOU WEREN'T EVEN THERE!

OKAY, HONEY, I DON'T HAVE TO BE TOLD TWICE!
JULIE!
BRUCE!
THAT WOMAN WILL MAKE A PERFECT FIRST VICTIM!
BUT... SHE'S JUST A DAME, BOSS! WOULDN'T IT BE BETTER TO...
IDIOT! HAVE YOU LEARNED NOTHING SINCE I PLUCKED YOU OUT OF THE SMALLVILLE JUVENILE DETENTION HOME?
SO-CALLED INNOCENT VICTIMS ARE ALWAYS BEST. THEIR DEATHS CREATE THE GREATEST TERROR.
NOW, LET THE SNAP OF BONE AND SPURT OF BLOOD BE A SIGN TO ALL OF METROPOLIS THAT...
EH..??
SOMETHING IS STOPPING THE ROBOT !?!

WHO ..??
SUPERMAN!!

OH-HH!!
HE CRUSHED THE ROBOT INTO A SPHERE WITH HIS BARE HANDS!
HEY! WHAT DO YOU THINK YOU'RE DOING?
"THAT ROBOT WAS PRIVATE PROPERTY!"
ER...
AH...

INCREDIBLE!
WHAT A MAN!!
BRUCE...
"...WHY CAN'T YOU BE MORE LIKE HIM?"
I WAS BEGINNING TO THINK JULIE WOULD NEVER GET TIRED ENOUGH TO WANT TO SLEEP.
THERE WAS MORE TO THAT ROBOT RUNNING AMOK THAN A SIMPLE ELECTRONIC MALFUNCTION.
IT WENT AFTER JULIE WITH INTENT!

THE FAIR WILL BE CLOSING FOR THE NIGHT IN JUST A FEW MINUTES...
...AND THE PAVILION THAT HAD "ELECTROX" ON DISPLAY IS ALREADY DESERTED.
WHICH MAKES IT THE PERFECT PLACE TO START MY...
I DON'T KNOW ABOUT THIS, LOIS!
BRIBING THAT GUARD TO LET US IN... THAT DOESN'T SEEM LIKE SOMETHING THE CHIEF WOULD APPROVE OF!
GEORGE TAYLOR APPROVES OF ANYTHING THAT GETS SCOOPS FOR THE STAR, KENT.
AND WE WOULDN'T HAVE TO BE SNEAKING AROUND LIKE THIS...
...IF YOU BEING LATE--AS USUAL --HADN'T MADE ME MISS ALL THE EXCITEMENT!
SAY...! WHAT DO YOU SUPPOSE THIS IS..?
SOMETHING BETTER LEFT FOR AN EXPERT TO EXAMINE, MISS LANE.

WELL, EXCUSE ME IF I DON'T GO ALL WEAK IN THE KNEES, FRIEND, BUT YOU'RE SMALL POTATOES IN THIS TOWN. IT TAKES MORE THAN A SPOOK ACT TO OUTDO SUPERMAN!

YOUR HOMEGROWN HERO IS IMPRESSIVE, MISS LANE...

...BUT THIS JOB REQUIRES BRAINS, NOT BRAWN.

HEY!!

NOT SO FAST THERE, FELLA!

CLUMSY, KENT.

AND I DON'T HAVE TIME FOR THIS...
OW!!
COME BACK HERE, YOU!
KENT! ARE YOU ..?
I'M... UHN... OKAY, LOIS.
BUT I HAD TO PRETEND TO BE HURT--THAT BLOW WOULD HAVE NEAR CRIPPLED A NORMAL MAN!
ELECT
FINE! NEXT TIME REMIND ME TO TELL OUR EDITOR I DON'T NEED TO BE BABYSITTING YOU WHEN I'M COVERING A STORY!
NOW THE BAT-MAN HAS VANISHED!
HEY! WHAT ARE YOU TWO DOING IN THERE? THAT PAVILION IS CLOSED!
WE'RE JUST THE LAST ONES OUT, OFFICER.
NOTHING TO BE ALARMED ABOUT!
PLAY IT SMOOTH AS YOU LIKE, KENT, BUT I'M GOING TO KEEP AN EYE ON YOU!
YOU WENT DOWN EASILY ENOUGH, BUT HITTING YOUR NECK WAS LIKE HITTING A STEEL GIRDER!
GHOUSE

"I WONDER IF THERE MIGHT BE MORE THAN ONE ROBOT WANDERING AROUND HERE..?"
FOOLS!!
I WARNED YOU NOT TO LEAVE ANY TRACES OF YOUR ACTIONS WHEN YOU PLANTED THE REMOTE CONTROL DEVICE ON ELECTROX!
WHAT DID THAT NOSY REPORTER FIND?
IT COULDN'T HAVE BEEN ANYTHING, BOSS! I SWEPT THE AREA MYSELF!
IT WAS ENOUGH TO BE OF INTEREST TO THE BAT-MAN!
BLAST! MY PLANS WERE FINELY CALCULATED TO ALLOW FOR OCCASIONAL INTERFERENCE BY SUPERMAN...
"...BUT I HAD NOT ANTICIPATED ANOTHER COSTUMED INTERLOPER!!"
I'M STILL NOT SATISFIED, BRUCE! I WANT TO KNOW WHERE YOU SNUCK OFF TO IN THE MIDDLE OF THE NIGHT!
I TOLD YOU, HONEY, I JUST NEEDED TO TAKE A WALK. TOO MUCH EXCITEMENT FOR ME TO SLEEP, I GUESS.
LET'S TALK ABOUT IT LATER--HERE'S ROOM SERVICE WITH OUR BREAKFAST...
1017
...BUT I DON'T SEE HOW YOU CAN GET THROUGH YOUR MORNING ON A BAGEL AND A CUP OF COFFEE, LOIS!
AND A CIGARETTE, KENT! DON'T FORGET THE CIGARETTES! PACKED WITH NUTRITIONAL VALUE!
STEAK 'N' EGGS 35¢
BURGER 'N' CHIPS 30¢
WHAT ABOUT YOU? SEEMS LIKE THOSE KANSAS-STYLE BIG BREAKFASTS YOU POUND DOWN WOULD PUT YOU TO SLEEP FOR A WEEK!
I HAVE A RAPID METABOLISM, LOIS. NOW, SHALL WE GET OVER TO THE FAIRGROUNDS?
ACME
SIMPS

"THERE ARE A FEW LEADS I WANT TO FOLLOW UP BEFORE THE MORNING RUSH...!"
THIS PLACE IS SO PEACEFUL BEFORE ALL THE PEOPLE ARRIVE, BRUCE.
IT WAS A GOOD IDEA TO STAY AT A HOTEL SO CLOSE.
MMM... PITY WE COULDN'T FIND ANYTHING BETTER THAN THAT THREE-STAR DUMP, THOUGH.
SAY, LOOK OVER HERE...
GRAYSONS
THE FLYING GRAYSONS.
THEY'RE SUPPOSED TO BE VERY GOOD.
APPEARING NITELY THRU SEPTEMBER
ESPECIALLY THAT YOUNG LAD OF THEIRS.
I'VE HEARD HE'S SOMETHING OF A BOY WONDER.
NOW, WHAT SAY WE HAVE A LOOK AT SOME OF THE AUTOMOTIVE EXHIBITS?
I'M IN THE MARKET FOR A NEW CAR.
LOOK! THAT'S BRUCE WAYNE! I HEARD HE ARRIVED YESTERDAY.
HM! TWO OF GOTHAM'S MOST FAMOUS SONS AT THE FAIR AT THE SAME TIME.
CONNECTION?
WHAT--YOU THINK MAYBE WAYNE IS THE BAT-MAN, KENT?
THAT'S ABOUT AS LIKELY AS YOU BEING SUPERMAN.
HA HA..! THAT'S A GOOD ONE, LOIS!
THOUGH NOW THAT YOU MENTION IT...

"...IT DOES SEEM MORE THAN A COINCIDENCE..."
THIS IS JUST TOO BORING FOR WORDS, BRUCE.
WHY DON'T YOU SPEND ANOTHER HOUR AND A HALF LOOKING AT CARS...
...WHILE I GO SEE THE REST OF THE FAIR!
HM? OH--WHATEVER YOU LIKE, HONEY. MEET YOU LATER FOR LUNCH..?
THAT TOOK LONGER THAN I ANTICIPATED. JULIE HAS A HIGHER TOLERANCE FOR BOREDOM THAN I GAVE HER CREDIT FOR!
THEY'RE SPLITTING UP.
YOU FOLLOW THE GIRL, LOIS--I'LL KEEP AN EYE ON WAYNE.
GOOD PLAN, KENT. JUST ONE REFINEMENT I WANT TO ADD.
"LET'S MAKE THAT THE OTHER WAY AROUND..."
HE'S HEADING FOR THE EASTINGHOUSE PAVILION. BUT THAT'S CLOSED WHILE THEY REPAIR THE DAMAGE DONE BY ELECTROX.
NOT THAT THAT SEEMS TO BE SLOWING DOWN OUR MR. WAYNE!
AJAX CORP
ORRY
OSED

THAT SCRAP OF METAL MISS LANE FOUND IS A SIGNIFICANT CLUE, SINCE NOTHING ELSE HERE SEEMS TO BE MADE OF THAT ALLOY.
GET IT RIGHT THIS TIME!
WITH THIS PLACE CLOSED, IT'S A PERFECT CHANCE-- OUR LAST--TO MAKE SURE THERE ARE NO CLUES LEFT!
DON'T PLAY THE BIG BOSS AROUND US, ELL. WE'VE SEEN YOU FOLD IN FRONT OF TH' ULTRA-HUMANITE.
WATCH YOUR LIP, ENN.
I PLAY TOADY TO ULTRA ONLY BECAUSE IT SUITS MY PURPOSES.
WELL, WELL! THE ULTRA-HUMANITE IS BACK IN METROPOLIS, EH?
JUST KNOWING HE'S AROUND IS THE BEST LEAD I COULD HOPE FOR.
GOT TO PHONE IT IN BEFORE KENT FINDS OUT ABOUT...
GOIN' SOME-WHERES, CUTIE?

YES--OUT OF HERE!
LOIS LANE!
STOP HER!
BLAST! THERE'S NO WAY I CAN CHANGE TO THE BAT-MAN...
I'LL JUST HAVE TO DEPEND ON NOT BEING RECOGNIZED...
HEY!!
WHO THE HECK IS THIS GUY..??
THE SAME ONE WHO SEEMED DETERMINED TO STAND UP TO ELECTROX, YESTERDAY.
THIS NEURO-STUNNER WILL FIX HIS WAGON!
TZZAP

TAKE HIM DOWN TO THE RIVER AND DUMP HIM.
I'M GOING TO TAKE THE GIRL BACK TO ULTRA. HE'LL WANT TO FIND OUT HOW MUCH SHE KNOWS.
RIGHT!

MAYBE WE SHOULD CHECK THIS GUY'S WALLET--FIND OUT WHO HE IS?
WE CAN HELP OURSELVES TO HIS CASH, ANYWAY. WITH THREADS LIKE THESE, HE'S PROB'LY CARRYIN' QUITE A ROLL...

WELL, WELL! LOOKIT THIS! HE'S THAT FANCY GOTHAM BIG SHOT, BRUCE WAYNE!
WAYNE? HEY--HE'D BE WORTH MORE ALIVE THAN AS FISHFOOD...
SAY... WHAT'S GOING ON OVER THERE?

THAT'S ME! YOU'RE LUCKY I HAPPENED BY, MISTER!
WHO ARE YOU? AND WHY WERE THOSE CREEPS DUSTING YOU DOWN?

JUST SOMEONE WHO HAPPENED TO BE IN THE WRONG PLACE AT THE RIGHT TIME, DICK.
THANKS FOR YOUR HELP.

"I WON'T FORGET YOU!!"
I DIDN'T NOTIFY THE POLICE ABOUT THE ATTACK ON BRUCE WAYNE, OR LOIS LANE'S KIDNAPPING.
DESPITE THE ASSERTIONS OF THOSE TWO I MET WHEN I LANDED, THE POLICE HERE MAY WELL BE JUST AS CORRUPT AS THEY ARE IN GOTHAM.
BUT THIS "ULTRA-HUMANITE" IS NOT LIKELY TO LEAVE THAT TRUCK FOR THEM TO FIND, EITHER WAY.

SOMEONE IS BOUND TO COME TO RETRIEVE IT...
GOOD... THE TRUCK'S STILL HERE.

NOW TO GET OUT OF HERE BEFORE...

UH-HHR...
WHERE..??
HAVE A NICE NAP?
NOW... LET'S CHAT.

NO! PLEASE! HELP ME!

TELL ME!

PLEASE!!

NOOOOOOOOH!!

CAREFUL THERE, FELLA!
YOU SHOULDN'T EVEN BE WORKING UP HERE, THIS TIME OF...
YOU!
SUPERMAN!
IF I'D KNOWN YOU WERE THERE TO CATCH HIM, I WOULDN'T HAVE LET HIM FALL!

HUH!
IF I'D KNOWN YOU LET HIM FALL, I WOULDN'T HAVE CAUGHT HIM.
SHALL I TOSS HIM OFF AGAIN?
NO!
I'LL TALK! I'LL TALK!

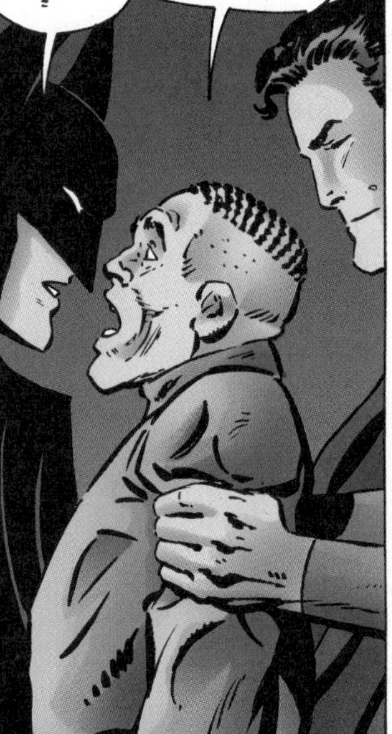

"I THINK THERE IS..!"
Prosperity Plaza
THIS IS THE PLACE.
YES-- THERE'S A CONCEALED HATCH HERE.
ULTRA HAS BEEN HIDING RIGHT IN THE MIDDLE OF THE FAIR!
THE BAT-MAN!

AND DON'T FOR-GET ME, OLD PAL...
BAH! I HAVE NO TIME TO WASTE ON THE LIKES OF YOU!
BLAST! HE'S BUILT A ROCKET SHIP INTO THE PYRAMAX!
AND SOME-THING ELSE!
THIS DIAL IS READING OFF SOME KIND OF... COUNTDOWN.
ULTRA LEFT A LITTLE SURPRISE TO COVER HIS ESCAPE!
HE'S RIGGED THE HYPERGLOBE TO EXPLODE!

BUT IF I TIME THIS RIGHT...
...I CAN KILL TWO BIRDS...
"...WITH ONE STONE!!"

The Beginning...

1949
FamilyMatters

LAUGH ALL YOU WANT, JOKER. YOU'RE IN METROPOLIS NOW, AND IN METROPOLIS WE EAT THE LIKES OF YOU FOR LUNCH!
OH, DO YOU, MRS. KENT? DO YOU INDEED?
WELL, MAYBE SUPERMAN HAS JUST HAD IT EASY ALL THESE YEARS. MAYBE HE'S NEVER HAD TO FACE ANYONE WITH A REAL TALENT FOR EVIL!
I'M SURE WE'LL FIND OUT SOON ENOUGH, JOKER. MY HUSBAND WILL HAVE CONTACTED SUPERMAN BY NOW, AND...
YOUR HUSBAND, MRS. KENT?
OR, WOULD YOU PREFER... MRS. SUPERMAN..?
OH, NOT THAT AGAIN! YOU'RE BEHIND THE TIMES, JOKER. NO ONE IN METROPOLIS HAS THOUGHT CLARK WAS SUPERMAN SINCE THE DAY WE GOT MARRIED.
IZZAT SO?
WELL, MY SOURCES ARE OF ANOTHER OPINION, LOIS--MAY I CALL YOU LOIS?
LET'S KEEP IT "MRS. KENT," SHALL WE?

I DON'T KNOW WHAT PART OF YOUR MADNESS BROUGHT YOU TO MY TURF, JOKER...
...BUT YOU MAKE A BIG MISTAKE WHEN YOU MESS WITH MY FRIENDS!
THE GUEST OF HONOR!
AT LAST!
YOU LIVE UP TO YOUR PRESS, SUPERMAN!
NOT AS IMPRESSIVE AS BATMAN, OF COURSE--BUT THEN YOU DON'T NEED TO BE, DO YOU? ALL THOSE FANCY POWERS TAKE AWAY THE NEED FOR PANACHE!
WHATEVER YOU LIKE, JOKER.
YOU'LL HAVE PLENTY OF TIME TO THINK ABOUT IT, IN PRISON.
YOU KNOW, SUPERMAN... I DON'T THINK SO.
SAY "HI" TO AN OL' FRIEND!

GREEN KRYPTON-ITE!
SUPERMAN! FLY AWAY WHILE YOU STILL CAN!
TOO LATE FOR THAT, MRS. S!

THIS ISN'T MERELY KRYPTONITE. IT'S AN ESPECIALLY POTENT LITTLE ROCK CREATED IN THE LAB OF A FRIEND OF MINE.
THIS LAB, IN FACT!
CONCEN-TRATED... KRYPTON-ITE...!
JOKER... YOU FIEND...

YOU SAY THAT AS IF IT'S A BAD THING, SUPERDUPES!
ME, ON THE OTHER HAND, I THINK FIENDISHNESS IS SORELY UNDERRATED AS A...

WHAT IN..?
GAME OVER, JOKER.

NO! IT CAN'T BE! YOU SHOULDN'T EVEN BE ABLE TO MOVE..!
A SLIGHT MISCALCULA-TION ON YOUR PART, JOKER.
NOW...

UNGH!

SUPERMAN!!

WELL! IT'S ABOUT TIME! I MAY NEVER BE ABLE TO USE THIS **WRIST** AGAIN!

SPARE ME YOUR **WHINING**, JOKER. I COULD NOT **ACT** UNTIL I WAS **CERTAIN** OF THE RESULT.

LUTHOR!

CONFUSED, READER?

DON'T BE! EVERYTHING WILL BECOME CRYSTAL CLEAR IN DUE TIME!
AND FOR THE BEGINNING OF OUR ANSWER, WE MUST FIRST LOOK BACK IN TIME, A PERIOD OF SOME TWENTY-FOUR HOURS, TO THE FAMOUS UNDERGROUND HEADQUARTERS OF GOTHAM CITY'S MOST FAMOUS CRIMEFIGHTER!
HE'S ALL PACKED, SIR. HE SEEMS QUITE DETERMINED TO GO.
THANK YOU, ALFRED.
AREN'T YOU GOING TO GO UP, SIR? I SAW THE BAT-SIGNAL, BUT HE'LL BE GONE IN JUST A FEW MINUTES.
I HAVE ALREADY SUMMONED A TAXI.
HE... KNOWS WHERE I AM, IF HE WANTS TO SAY GOODBYE, ALFRED. IF LEAVING FOR COLLEGE IS MORE IMPORTANT THAN ANSWERING GORDON'S CALL...

MASTER BRUCE... IF I MAY SPEAK FREELY--YOU HAVE KNOWN FOR MONTHS THAT THIS TIME MUST COME.
TRULY, SINCE YOU ADOPTED MASTER DICK NINE YEARS AGO, WE HAVE BOTH KNOWN THERE MUST COME A TIME WHEN THE ROBIN WOULD FLY THE NEST.
I... KNOW THAT, OLD FRIEND. BUT IT DOESN'T MAKE IT EASIER, NOW THAT THE TIME HAS FINALLY COME.
REMEMBER WHAT SUPERMAN SAID, ALFRED? HOW HE WONDERED ALOUD IF I'D "CLEANED UP MY ACT" BECAUSE OF HAVING A KID IN TOW?
MASTER DICK DID SEEM TO HELP YOU DAMP DOWN YOUR DEMONS, SIR.
FUNNY... WHEN I FIRST BECAME BATMAN--BAT-MAN AS I WAS THEN--IT NEVER OCCURRED TO ME I'D WANT OR NEED A PARTNER IN MY WAR ON CRIME.
NOW, IT'S HARD TO IMAGINE HOW I'LL FUNCTION WITHOUT HIM!
YOU'LL DO JUST FINE, BRUCE!
MASTER DICK! YOUR TAXI...
I CALLED AND CANCELED IT, ALFRED. THERE'LL BE LOTS OF OTHER CABS...

"...BUT ONLY ONE CHANCE FOR BATMAN AND ROBIN TO GO INTO ACTION FOR THE LAST TIME!!"
YOU CALLED COMMISSIONER?
BATMAN! ROBIN! I WAS BEGINNING TO THINK YOU WEREN'T COMING!
WE HAD A SLIGHT DELAY.
WHAT'S UP?
A BREAK-IN AT THE GOTHAM METALLURGICAL INSTITUTE.
I WOULD NOT HAVE CALLED ON THE TWO OF YOU, ORDINARILY, BUT A WITNESS REPORTED SEEING A MAN WITH GREEN HAIR...
THE JOKER!!
THEN... HE'S NOT DEAD!
ANTHONY
IT WAS ASKING TOO MUCH TO HOPE THAT HE WAS, ROBIN.
AND SINCE IT'S FOUR YEARS SINCE WE THOUGHT HE DIED IN THAT NUCLEAR BLAST...
"...THERE'S NO TELLING WHAT NEW MADNESS HE MAY HAVE BREWING..!!"
TONY GORDON STILL SEEMS RETICENT ABOUT CALLING ON US FOR HELP, BATMAN.
I DON'T THINK HE WAS EVER REALLY COMFORTABLE WITH THE FACT THAT IT WAS MY ENDORSEMENT THAT FINALLY SWUNG THE PEOPLE OF GOTH-AM IN HIS FAVOR WHEN HE TOOK OVER HIS FATHER'S JOB.
GOTHAM M.I.
GOTHAM M
INSTITU

YES... LOSING JIM GORDON WAS ONE OF THE WORST BLOWS GOTHAM HAS EVER HAD TO ENDURE...
THERE ARE THE INVESTIGATING POLICE OFFICERS. LET'S SEE WHAT WE CAN FIND OUT ABOUT THE JOKER'S SUDDEN INTEREST IN METALLURGY.
BATMAN AND ROBIN! GLAD YOU COULD MAKE IT!

THE JOKER AND HIS MEN DID A PRETTY THOROUGH JOB OF WRECKING THIS PLACE.
IF THEY WERE TRYING TO COVER WHAT IT WAS THEY STOLE, THEY'VE SUCCEEDED!
WHY WOULD JOKER WORRY ABOUT HIDING WHAT HE STOLE?
WE DO SOME DELICATE SECRET WORK HERE, ROBIN.
I THINK THAT MAY BE WHAT INTERESTED THE JOKER.

JOKER HAS ONLY ONE INTEREST, MISS--MAKING HIMSELF RICH.
WERE YOU WORKING ON ANYTHING OF GREAT FINANCIAL WORTH?
NO, BATMAN. IN FACT, I CHECKED THE INVENTORY, AND THIS IS ONE OF THOSE RARE WEEKS WHEN WE DON'T EVEN HAVE ANY PRECIOUS METALS IN STOCK.

YET YOU HAD SOMETHING THAT WOULD ATTRACT THE JOKER...
AND I THINK I'VE JUST FOUND IT...

COME ON, ROBIN...

"...WE HAVE A TRIP TO MAKE!"
METROPOLIS?
YOU'RE GONNA HAVE TO CONNECT THOSE DOTS FOR ME, BATMAN!
WHAT GETS US FROM THE JOKER'S HEIST TO NEEDING TO CONTACT SUPERMAN?
A BIT OF A STRETCH OF MY POWERS OF DEDUCTIVE REASONING TO BE SURE, OLD CHUM...
...BUT WHILE THERE WAS NOTHING INTRINSICALLY VALUABLE ON THAT LIST...
...I DID SPOT THE SYMBOL FOR SOMETHING THAT COULD BE VERY DANGEROUS IN THE WRONG HANDS.
AND HANDS DON'T GET MUCH WRONGER THAN THE JOKER'S, EH, BATMAN?
SUPERMAN! THEN THE MESSAGE I SENT TO CLARK KENT AT THE DAILY PLANET GOT THROUGH AS I'D INTENDED.
AND NOT A MOMENT TOO SOON, BATMAN.
IF YOUR WARNING HAD COME EVEN A FEW MINUTES LATER, IT MIGHT HAVE MEANT DISASTER!
YOU SEE...

"...LOIS HAS BEEN KIDNAPPED BY THE JOKER AND LEX LUTHOR!"
WHICH BRINGS US BACK TO THE HERE AND NOW...
"...AND RETURN THE KRYPTONITE TO ITS LEAD CONTAINER.
"I DO NOT WANT SUPERMAN KILLED WHEN HE FINALLY ARRIVES."
THAT'S WAY TOO CREEPY, SUPERMAN! YOU DON'T HAVE TO DO LUTHOR'S VOICE WHEN YOU REPEAT WHAT YOUR SUPERHEARING HAS PICKED UP!
IT LOOKS LIKE "PLAN A" HAS COME OUT SOMEWHAT LESS SUCCESSFULLY THAN WE MIGHT HAVE HOPED.
I'M GOING TO HAVE TO GO IN THERE AFTER ALL..!
NO, WAIT A SECOND!
"THERE MAY BE ANOTHER WAY TO DO THIS..!"
DEAD! BATMAN IS DEAD!
I ONLY WISH IT COULD HAVE BEEN MORE DIRECTLY BY MY HAND!
I DON'T UNDERSTAND WHAT YOU HAVE TO DO WITH ANY OF THIS, JOKER!
WHY ARE YOU IN METROPOLIS? AND WHY ARE YOU SO CHUMMY WITH LUTHOR?
THE JOKER OWES ME, MRS. KENT. AND, ODDLY ENOUGH, THE JOKER IS A MAN WHO ALWAYS REPAYS HIS DEBTS.
HE "OWES" YOU? FOR WHAT?
FOR FREEING ME, LOIS.
FOR RETURNING ME TO THE UNITED STATES AFTER ALMOST FOUR YEARS IN A SOVIET SLAVE LABOR CAMP!
THAT ON TOP OF SIX MONTHS AS A "GUEST" OF THE THIRD REICH!

WHEN I LEARNED OF THE JOKER'S CONDITION AND WHEREABOUTS, I REALIZED HIS INTIMATE KNOWLEDGE OF GOTHAM CITY WOULD SERVE ME WELL IN THE OBTAINING OF AN ELEMENT NECESSARY TO MY PLAN!
WHAT ELEMENT?
YOU DIDN'T NEED THE JOKER TO FIND THAT GREEN K. THERE ARE TONS OF THE STUFF ALL OVER THE WORLD!

INDEED THERE ARE, MRS. KENT. AND I HAVE AVAILED MYSELF OF THEM IN THE PAST.
BUT FOR THIS PARTICULAR SCHEME I NEEDED SOMETHING ELSE.
SOMETHING VERY RARE.

"TO THAT END, I KNEW PROVIDENCE WAS SMILING ON ME WHEN I LEARNED IN THE SAME WEEK OF A SAMPLE BEING STUDIED IN GOTHAM...
"...AND THE LOCATION OF THE VERY MAN WHO COULD STEAL IT FOR ME!

"THUS, MOBILIZING MY WORLD WIDE RESOURCES, I ENGINEERED AN ASSAULT ON THE SIBERIAN CAMP WHERE THE JOKER WAS BEING HELD...

"THE MUCH-VAUNTED MIGHT OF THE SOVIET ARMY WAS AS NOTHING TO MY OWN 'SOLDIERS'...

"WITH MY TARGET ACQUIRED WE LEFT THAT FROZEN WASTELAND...
"...AND A FEW WEEKS LATER, HAD THE JOKER BACK UP TO HIS FIGHTING STRENGTH!"
ALL RIGHT, LUTHOR--I OWE YOU BIG TIME!
TELL ME WHAT YOU WANT.
WHAT I WANT, JOKER, IS A SMALL PIECE OF YELLOW METAL...
I MUST CONFESS, I WAS NERVOUS ABOUT USING THE JOKER'S UNIQUE TALENTS. HIS APPROACH TO CRIME HAS ALWAYS BEEN, SHALL WE SAY, MORE FLAMBOYANT THAN MY OWN.
QUIT YOUR GRUMBLING, LUTHOR. I GOT THE JOB DONE, DIDN'T I? AND WITHOUT ANY FUSS OR MUSS!
EXCEPT THAT YOU WERE SPOTTED, JOKER.

SUPER-MAN!
AND CLEARLY THE REAL ONE THIS TIME!
ENOUGH GAMES, LUTHOR.
YOUR SCHEME IS JUST TOO CLEVER FOR ME, THIS TIME.
LET MY WIFE GO, AND YOU CAN DO WHATEVER YOU WANT WITH ME.
CLARK! NO!
HOW VERY NOBLE.
UNFORTUNATELY, MY PLAN WOULD LACK A CERTAIN DEGREE OF SATISFACTION IF YOUR SPOUSE WAS NOT HERE TO WITNESS YOUR HUMILIATION, SUPERMAN.
HOWEVER--SINCE YOU SO GRA-CIOUSLY AC-KNOWLEDGE ME AS YOUR BETTER, I WILL ALLOW HER TO WATCH FROM BEHIND THIS LEAD SHIELD.
YOUR UNBORN OFF-SPRING WILL COME TO NO FURTHER HARM!

FURTHER HARM?
WHAT ARE YOU TALKING ABOUT, LUTHOR? WHAT HAVE YOU DONE TO HIM??
NOTHING, DEAR FELLOW! NOTHING! I MERELY REFER TO THE DISCOMFORT THE LITTLE TYKE MUST HAVE FELT WHEN THE JOKER EXPOSED THE GREEN K!

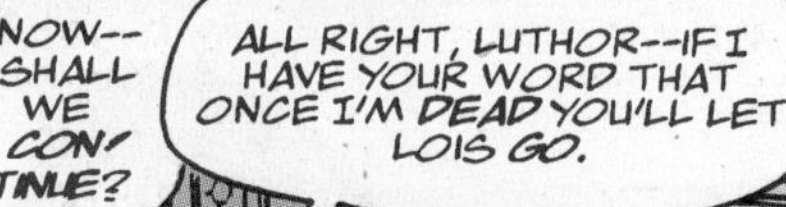
NOW--SHALL WE CON-TINUE?
ALL RIGHT, LUTHOR--IF I HAVE YOUR WORD THAT ONCE I'M DEAD YOU'LL LET LOIS GO.

CLARK! NO! DON'T DO IT!!

ONCE AGAIN YOU MISS THE POINT, SUPERMAN.
IT IS NOT YOUR DEATH I CRAVE HERE. DEAD, YOU WOULD NOT BE ABLE TO EXPERIENCE THE FRUSTRATION AND IMPOTENCE AS YOU WATCH ME TAKE OVER THE WORLD!

FOR TEN YEARS YOU'VE BEEN A THORN IN MY SIDE, SUPERMAN. ANY OTHER SUPERHERO I COULD HAVE SWAT-TED AS EASILY AS I DID BATMAN.
ONLY YOU HAVE EVER BEEN A THREAT TO ME.
SPARE ME THE SPEECH-ES, LUTHOR.
JUST GET ON WITH IT.

SUCH EAGERNESS TO BECOME A MERE MORTAL, SUPERMAN!
I WONDER, HAVE YOU PERHAPS GROWN WEARY OF THE CONSTANT DEMANDS MADE ON YOU BY A TROUBLED WORLD?
VERY WELL--LET ME RELIEVE YOU OF THAT BURDEN FOREVER!!

EVEN THE MOST BRIEF EXPOSURE TO THIS GOLD KRYPTONITE AND YOUR POWERS WILL BE GONE FOR...
AH-GH!!!
YOU MELTED THE BOX WITH YOUR HEAT VISION!!
LIAR!! YOU GAVE YOUR WORD YOU WOULD DO NOTHING TO STOP ME!
AND I DIDN'T, LUTHOR.
BUT I DID!
ANOTHER ONE..?!?
THE REAL ONE, THIS TIME, JOKER.
AFTER ALL, IF WE COULD FOOL YOU ONCE, WHY NOT A SECOND TIME?

GOING SOME-WHERE, JOKER?

NO! IT CAN'T BE!

SURE IT CAN!

VERY WELL, SUPERMAN... YOU HAVE **BEATEN** ME AGAIN. BUT A **WISE** MAN CAN SNATCH HIS OWN KIND OF **VICTORY** EVEN FROM THE JAWS OF DEFEAT!

UNGH! THE GREEN KRYPTON-ITE!

YES... AND WITH YOU NOW **POWERLESS**, SUPERMAN, MY **GUN** IS ENOUGH TO HOLD BATMAN AND ROBIN AT BAY WHILE I MAKE MY **EXIT**.

A DEPARTURE YOU MAY FIND **REMINISCENT** OF THE **FIRST TIME** WE **THREE** CROSSED PATHS...

FAREWELL, FOOLS!

I THINK WE SHALL NOT MEET AGAIN!

I THINK WE'D BETTER GET OUT OF HERE, SUPERMAN!
IF I TAKE LUTHOR'S MEANING CORRECTLY...
...HIS INTENDED MEANS OF DEPARTURE WILL BE EXPLOSIVE!

LUTHOR WILL HAVE COOKED HIMSELF AND THE JOKER IN THAT!
MAYBE, ROBIN. BUT I WOULD NOT BET MY LIFE ON IT!
AND SPEAKING OF YOUR LIFE, BATMAN...
WHY AREN'T YOU DEAD?
WE KNEW LUTHOR WAS HIDING IN THERE SOMEWHERE, LOIS...
...BUT HE'S HONEYCOMBED THE LAB WITH LEAD-LINED PASSAGEWAYS.
HE COULD BE IN ANY OF THEM!
WHICH MEANS THE FIRST THING WE HAVE TO DO IS LURE HIM OUT OF HIDING!
AND I THINK I KNOW JUST THE WAY TO DO THAT!
"SO, WHEN LUTHOR SHOT BATMAN, I USED MY HEAT VISION TO VAPORIZE THE BULLET...
"...PLUS A PUFF OF MY SUPER BREATH TO KNOCK BATMAN OVER."
IT REQUIRED SPLIT-SECOND TIMING, BUT SUPERMAN IS GOOD AT THAT!
THEN, ALL I HAD TO DO WAS USE AN OLD TIBETAN METHOD TO STOP MY HEART...
AND WE ALL THOUGHT YOU WERE DEAD!
BUT... WHY THE CHARADES?
WHY NOT JUST MELT ALL THE LEAD BOXES? YOU MUST HAVE GUESSED THAT WAS WHERE THE KRYPTONITE WOULD BE.
WE DID--BUT I ALSO SAW THAT LUTHOR HAD BOOBY-TRAPPED THEM. IF I'D TRIED ANYTHING BEFORE HE DEACTIVATED THE TRAPS, THE WHOLE ROOM WOULD HAVE BEEN SPRAYED WITH KRYPTONITE SHRAPNEL!

I GUESS THAT COVERS IT--EXCEPT FOR SOMETHING LUTHOR SAID ABOUT OUR UNBORN CHILD BEING HARMED BY THE GREEN K RADIATION.
SURELY... I WOULD HAVE FELT THAT, THE FIRST TIME THE JOKER PULLED OUT THE KRYPTONITE?
YOU CERTAINLY SHOULD HAVE, LOIS, UNLESS...
SUPER-MAN? WHAT IS IT?
LUTHOR MUST HAVE EXPOSED LOIS TO THE GOLD K BEFORE WE ARRIVED.
MY X-RAY VISION REVEALS THE BABY'S ATOMIC STRUCTURE HAS BEEN PERMANENTLY REALIGNED.
"HE'S COMPLETELY HUMAN NOW..."
I... SUPPOSE IT'S NOT THE END OF THE WORLD. AS LONG AS THE BABY ISN'T HURT IN SOME WAY...
THERE ARE WORSE THINGS, AFTER ALL, THAN GROWING UP HUMAN!
MAYBE--BUT GROWING UP THE HUMAN SON OF SUPERMAN?
WE HAVE ONLY ONE CHOICE, DON'T WE?
LITTLE JOEL MUST NEVER KNOW THAT HIS FATHER IS SUPERMAN!
THAT'S GOING TO BE... HARD TO PULL OFF, LOIS!
ALMOST IMPOSSIBLE, IN FACT, DICK. BUT LOIS IS RIGHT. IT'S THE ONLY SOLUTION...
IT MAY PROVE THE MOST DIFFICULT CHALLENGE OF YOUR CAREER AS SUPERMAN, CLARK.
BUT I CAN'T THINK OF A BETTER MAN--AND WOMAN--FOR THE JOB!

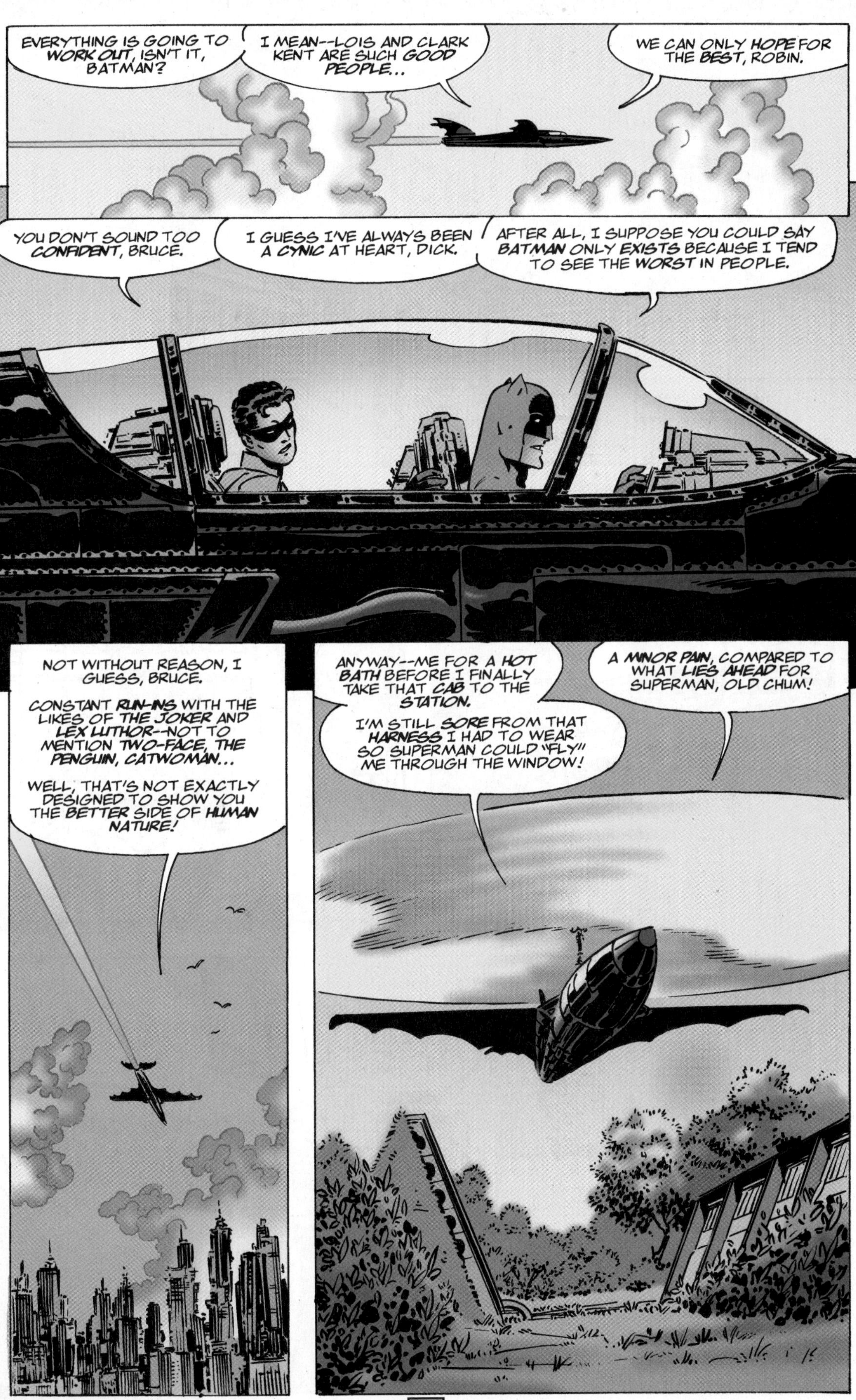
EVERYTHING IS GOING TO WORK OUT, ISN'T IT, BATMAN?
I MEAN--LOIS AND CLARK KENT ARE SUCH GOOD PEOPLE...
WE CAN ONLY HOPE FOR THE BEST, ROBIN.
YOU DON'T SOUND TOO CONFIDENT, BRUCE.
I GUESS I'VE ALWAYS BEEN A CYNIC AT HEART, DICK.
AFTER ALL, I SUPPOSE YOU COULD SAY BATMAN ONLY EXISTS BECAUSE I TEND TO SEE THE WORST IN PEOPLE.
NOT WITHOUT REASON, I GUESS, BRUCE.
CONSTANT RUN-INS WITH THE LIKES OF THE JOKER AND LEX LUTHOR--NOT TO MENTION TWO-FACE, THE PENGUIN, CATWOMAN...
WELL, THAT'S NOT EXACTLY DESIGNED TO SHOW YOU THE BETTER SIDE OF HUMAN NATURE!
ANYWAY--ME FOR A HOT BATH BEFORE I FINALLY TAKE THAT CAB TO THE STATION.
I'M STILL SORE FROM THAT HARNESS I HAD TO WEAR SO SUPERMAN COULD "FLY" ME THROUGH THE WINDOW!
A MINOR PAIN, COMPARED TO WHAT LIES AHEAD FOR SUPERMAN, OLD CHUM!

"I'M GLAD I'VE NEVER HAD TO FACE SUCH A TRIAL!!"
ONE YEAR LATER...
AND HOW ARE YOU THIS MORNING, MY LITTLE FRIENDS?
PLENTY OF HONEY FOR MASTER BRUCE AND HIS NEW BRIDE..?

AND NOT SO NEW ANY-MORE!
HARD TO BELIEVE THEY'VE BEEN MARRIED FOR OVER SIX MONTHS NOW!
GOOD MORN-ING, ALFRED.

GOOD MORNING, MADAM! DID YOU SLEEP WELL?
I WAS FINE UNTIL I WOKE UP--THEN IT WAS A BIT DICEY! HAVE YOU SEEN BRUCE THIS MORNING?

HE HAD TO GO INTO THE CITY ON URGENT BUSINESS, BUT HE SHOULD BE HOME BY NOON, MA'AM.
GOOD... ASK HIM TO COME TO MY STUDY WHEN HE GETS HOME, WOULD YOU?
I HAVE... SOMETHING IMPORTANT TO TELL HIM..!

1959
Strange Days
I AM DEFINITELY GETTING TOO OLD FOR THIS KIND OF THING!!
ACME

ALL RIGHT... ENOUGH MOANING!
IT'S THIRTY MINUTES SINCE THAT BUILDING CAME TO "LIFE."
JUST BE THANKFUL NO ONE HAS BEEN KILLED YET!
THIS IS AS CLOSE AS I DARE GET. WHIRLYBAT SET TO HOVER...
BEEN A WHILE SINCE I TRIED A STUNT ANYTHING LIKE WHAT I HAVE IN MIND...
...BUT THE ONLY WAY I CAN DEAL WITH THIS INSANITY IS TO TREAT THAT WALKING WAREHOUSE AS THOUGH IT REALLY IS ALIVE...
...AND TRY TO BREAK IT LIKE I WOULD A BRONCO!

WELL, NOW I'VE SEEN EVERY THING!
BATMAN'S RIDING THAT THING LIKE A BAT-COWBOY!
IT'S WORKING! THE THING IS CALMING DOWN!
GPD
BATMAN! YOU DID IT!
MAYBE, COMMIS-SIONER. OR MAY-BE MY LITTLE "FRIEND" JUST GOT TIRED OF HIS GAME!
ALL RIGHT, BAT-MITE! YOUR SIGNATURE IS ALL OVER THIS!
SHOW YOURSELF!
YOU GOT THE RIGHT IDEA, BATTY-BOY...
JUST THE WRONG IMP!
OH, NO!!

AT THAT MOMENT, MILES FROM GOTHAM CITY, IN METROPOLIS...
NO, SUPERMAN, NO! PUT THAT FREIGHTER DOWN!
LOOKS LIKE IT'S WORKING, OLSEN!

YES... THE MENTALLO-HELMET SUPERMAN BROUGHT BACK FROM PLANET X IS ABLE TO PENETRATE THE MADNESS BROUGHT ON BY HIS EXPOSURE TO RED KRYPTONITE YESTERDAY!
GOOD THING HE SPENT MOST OF THE LAST TWENTY-FOUR HOURS UNDERWATER, WALKING HERE FROM ENGLAND!
YOU'RE RIGHT! IT HAS BEEN ALMOST EXACTLY TWENTY-FOUR HOURS SINCE BRAINIAC SPRANG THE RED K TRAP!
GREEN LANTERN HAS ALREADY CAPTURED THAT MARAUDING ALIEN...
...AND THE EFFECTS OF THE RED K SHOULD BE ENDING RIGHT ABOUT...
...NOW!
AND SINCE EVERY EXPOSURE TO RED KRYPTON-ITE PRODUCES A UNIQUE REACTION, THAT'S THE LAST WE'LL SEE OF THE SUPER-GIANT OF METROPOLIS!
OH-HH!!
"OH, THANK HEAVEN!"
THE SUBURBAN METROPOLIS HOME OF THE KENT FAMILY...
MOMMY! MOMMY! LOOK!
NOT RIGHT NOW, HONEY.
MOMMY IS WATCHING THE NEWS REPORT ABOUT SUPERMAN.

AND SO IT SEEMS YET ANOTHER THREAT TO THE MAN OF STEEL HAS BEEN OVERCOME...
...IN NO SMALL PART DUE TO THE PROMPT ACTION OF DAILY PLANET STAR REPORTER JAMES OLSEN!
UNCLE JIMMY HELPED OUT SUPERMAN AGAIN, HUH, MOMMY?
IT SURE LOOKS THAT WAY, HONEY.
NOW... WHAT WAS IT YOU WANTED TO SHOW ME?
CHANNEL 8
SMOKE SUPERS
MY FEET, MOMMY! LOOK AT MY FEET!
WHAT'S WRONG WITH THEM, SWEETIE? THEY LOOK FINE TO ME.
BUT, MOMMY... THEY'RE NOT TOUCHING THE GROUND!
OH, NO..!
"THANKS, JIM! THAT'S ONE MORE I OWE YOU!"
IT'S NOTHING, SUPER-MAN! AFTER ALL THE TIMES YOU'VE PULLED MY FAT OUT OF THE FIRE, I'D SAY I STILL OWE YOU!
WELL, AFTER TODAY, I'M PRE-PARED TO CALL US EVEN, JIM!
THAT'S JUST GREAT, MR. SUPER-MAN!
NOW YOU CAN HELP ME!
BAT-MITE ..??

WHILE BACK IN GOTHAM...
ALL RIGHT, MXYZPTLK! WHAT'S YOUR GAME?
SUPERMAN ISN'T HERE FOR YOU TO PESTER!
CAREFUL, BATMAN!
FROM WHAT I'VE READ, IF YOU GET THIS GUY MAD, HE COULD TURN US ALL INTO KANGAROOS OR SOMETHING!
HOW STAGGERINGLY UNORIGINAL!
THAT'S JUST THE SORT OF PALTRY THING ONE OF YOU HUMANS WOULD DO IF YOU HAD THE POWER OF MY FIFTH-DIMENSIONAL BRAIN!
SPARE US THE INSULTS, MXYZPTLK. WHY ARE YOU HERE?
SIMPLE, BAT-BRAIN...
I'M HAVING A CONTEST WITH A CERTAIN LITTLE FRIEND OF YOURS.
A CONTEST TO PROVE MY SUPERHERO IS BETTER THAN HIS!
WHAT ..??
"BAT-MITE...!!!

...STOP THIS AT ONCE!
AND TELL ME WHY YOU'RE HERE INSTEAD OF BOTHERING BATMAN!
I DON'T BOTHER BATMAN, MR. SUPERMAN! I HELP HIM!
I'M AS MUCH HIS PARTNER AS ROBIN WAS!
"BUT I'LL ANSWER YOUR QUESTION.
"YESTERDAY I WAS IN MY OWN DIMENSION, MINDING MY OWN BUSI-NESS, WHEN SUDDENLY..."
HEY! WHERE AM I??
"FLYING AROUND, I QUICKLY DISCOVERED THAT I WAS INSIDE AN ALIEN SPACESHIP.
"AND THAT I WAS NOT ALONE THERE!!"
MR. MXYZ-PTLK!
BAT-MITE! IS THIS YOUR DOING?
RETURN ME TO THE FIFTH DIMENSION AT ONCE!
HE CANNOT DO THAT.

IT WAS NOT THE ONE YOU CALL "BAT-MITE" WHO TRANSPORTED YOU TO OUR SHIP, MXYZPTLK.
WE DID THAT, BECAUSE WE NEED YOUR HELP.
HELP? WHY SHOULD I WANT TO HELP YOU?
WHAT'S IN IT FOR ME?
AND... WHO ARE YOU?
OUR NAMES WOULD HAVE NO MEANING TO YOU. BUT WE ARE SEEKERS FROM THE FOURTH PLANET OF A STAR THE EARTHLINGS CALL EPSILON ERIDANI.

"OURS WAS A *PEACEFUL* PLANET...
"...A *HIGH CULTURE* WHICH HAD LONG SINCE SET ASIDE THE WAYS OF *WAR* AND *VIOLENCE*."

"SADLY, THAT WAS TO PROVE OUR *UNDOING*...
"...AS ONE DAY THERE APPEARED IN THE SKIES ABOVE OUR WORLD THE *SPACE ARMADA* OF THE *BORTAN EMPIRE*.

"WE SENT OUR AMBASSADORS UP TO THE *FLAGSHIP* OF THE ARMADA, TO EXTEND THE HAND OF PEACE TO THESE NEWCOMERS.
"THE BORTANS HAD NO INTEREST IN ANYTHING WE HAD TO SAY TO THEM.

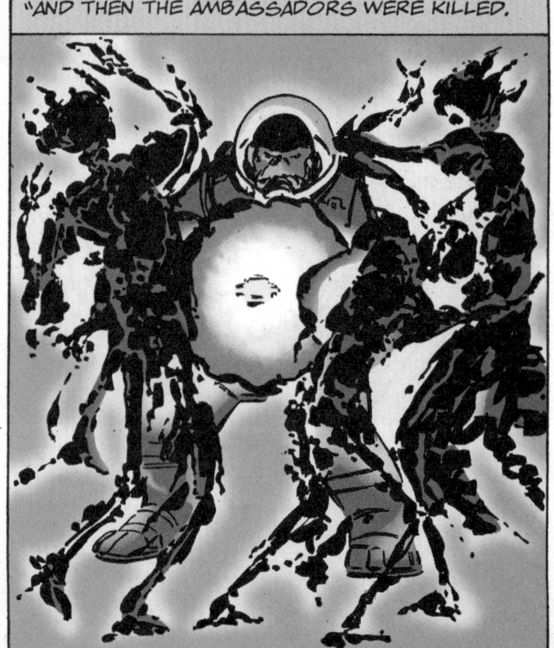

MY OWN FATHER WAS ONE OF THOSE AMBASSADORS.
"WITHIN DAYS, OUR CIVILIZATION HAD BEEN CRUSHED UNDER THE BORTAN BOOT.
"THE PEOPLE WERE HERDED INTO SLAVE LABOR CAMPS...
"...THOSE WHO DID NOT SUCCUMB TO AN EVEN WORSE FATE!
"BUT EVEN IN THOSE DARK DAYS THERE WERE POCKETS OF RESISTANCE.
"SEARCHING THE HEAVENS WITH STOLEN TECHNOLOGY, WE LEARNED OF EARTH...
"...AND OF THE BEINGS THE EARTHLINGS CALLED SUPERHEROES.

WE KNEW WHAT HAD TO BE DONE.

"USING EVERY SCRAP OF TECHNOLOGY WE COULD STEAL FROM THE BORTANS, WE BUILT A SMALL SPACE-SHIP.

"IT TOOK YEARS TO COMPLETE THE TASK.

"WITH LIMITED FUEL, ONLY TWO OF US COULD GO ON THIS MISSION OF HOPE...

"...AND ELUDING BORTAN FIGHTERS ON THE FRONTIER COST US DEARLY.

THERE'S NO NEED FOR TESTS! BATMAN IS THE GREATEST HERO EVER!
SEZ YOU! YOU DON'T THINK I'D WASTE MY TIME TORMENTING SUPERMAN IF HE WASN'T THE BEST THERE IS!
YES... FROM OUR STUDIES WE REALIZED EACH OF YOU WOULD THINK THUS...
...AND THAT YOUR POWERS WOULD MAKE YOU THE PERFECT TEST.
SHALL WE BEGIN..?

NOT SO FAST, CHROME-DOME!
I'LL BUY THAT THIS ALIEN TECHNOLOGY WAS ABLE TO PLUCK BAT-MIDGE AND ME FROM OUR DIMENSIONS...
...BUT THAT STILL DOESN'T TELL ME WHAT I HAVE TO GAIN BY HELPING YOU!
DON'T BE SO SELFISH, MXYZPTLK!

I'D BE PROUD TO HELP PROVE BATMAN IS THE GREATEST HERO, EVEN IF THESE PEOPLE DIDN'T NEED HELP!
YEAH, WELL, YOU ALWAYS WERE AN ANNOYING LITTLE DO-GOODER, BAT-BIT.
BUT I WANT TO GET ONE THING STRAIGHT. IF I PROVE TO YOU THAT SUPERMAN IS THE GREATEST... YOU TAKE HIM AWAY?
YES, WE WILL TRANSPORT THE WINNER TO OUR HOME ON THE OTHER SIDE OF THE UNIVERSE!

HEH HEH! IT WOULD TAKE SUPERSAP CENTURIES TO FLY BACK FROM THAT FAR AWAY!
OKAY, I'M IN! I'LL USE MY MAGIC TO PROVE SUPERMAN IS THE BEST!
AND I'LL SHOW YOU IT'S BATMAN WHO'S THE GREATEST CHAMPION!
WE THANK YOU...
BUT THERE IS A CONDITION WE MUST IMPOSE. WE REALIZE EACH OF YOU WILL WISH TO SEE HIS OWN CHOSEN SUPERHERO WIN...

"...SO EACH OF YOU MUST TEST THE OTHER'S CHAMPION!!"
I SEE--BUT THERE'S A TINY FLAW IN THIS SCHEME ISN'T THERE, BAT-MITE?
WHAT IF BATMAN AND I DON'T WANT TO BE "TESTED"?
SORRY, MR. SUPERMAN...
YOU DON'T HAVE ANY CHOICE!
OH, NO!!
HE'S BROUGHT TO LIFE THE MONSTER FROM THAT MOVIE BILLBOARD!!
"MOMMY, I'M SCARED!"

IT'S OKAY, KARA... THERE'S NOTHING TO BE AFRAID OF!
BUT WHY AM I FLOATING, MOMMY? JOEL NEVER FLOATS!

THAT'S BECAUSE YOUR BROTHER WAS EXPOSED TO GOLD KRYPTONITE RADIATION WHILE HE WAS STILL IN MY WOMB!
HE WAS BORN A NORMAL HUMAN BEING, BUT YOU, MY LITTLE LOVE, ARE HALF KRYPTONIAN!

WHICH IS WHY YOU NEED...
HERE IT IS!
THIS SHOULD TAKE CARE OF YOUR PROBLEM, HONEY!

OO, IT'S SO PRETTY, MOMMY! WHAT IS IT?
A SPECIAL JEWEL THAT WILL PUT YOU BACK ON THE GROUND AGAIN, KARA.
BUT YOU MUST PROMISE MOMMY YOU WON'T EVER TAKE IT OFF--OR TELL ANYBODY WHY YOU'RE WEARING IT!

OKAY, MOMMY!
THANKS!
YOU'RE WELCOME!
CLARK CREATED THAT AMULET FOR ME TO WEAR WHILE I WAS PREGNANT WITH KARA. IT EMITS RADIATION THAT MIMICS THE EFFECT OF A RED SUN.
IT PREVENTED KARA FROM DEVELOPING SUPERPOWERS WHILE SHE WAS STILL INSIDE ME...

"NOW IT WILL LET HER LEAD SOMETHING LIKE A NORMAL CHILDHOOD!!!"
YOUNG MASTER BRUCE..?
ARE YOU DOWN HERE?
OVER HERE, ALFRED.
OH, MY GOODNESS! YOUNG MASTER BRUCE... WHAT ARE YOU DOING??
NOTHING, REALLY.
I JUST THOUGHT I'D TRY THIS ON FOR SIZE. AFTER ALL, NEXT YEAR I'LL BE THE SAME AGE UNCLE DICK WAS WHEN HE BECAME ROBIN!
TRUE ENOUGH, YOUNG MASTER... BUT THOSE WERE DIFFERENT TIMES!
CHILDREN STILL LABORED IN THE MINES, OR WORKED IN SWEATSHOPS. NO ONE THOUGHT VERY MUCH ABOUT A TEN-YEAR-OLD CRIME-FIGHTER.
ESPECIALLY NOT MY DAD!
AND I KNOW MOM DOESN'T WANT ME TO EVEN THINK ABOUT BECOMING ROBIN UNTIL I'M AT LEAST EIGHTEEN.
BUT UNCLE DICK QUIT BEING ROBIN WHEN HE WAS NINETEEN!
YES--TO LEAVE US AND GO TO COLLEGE. AND NOW HE IS A LAWYER IN NEW YORK, FIGHTING CRIME IN A DIFFERENT WAY.

DAD NEVER TALKS ABOUT IT MUCH, BUT IT REALLY HURT HIM WHEN UNCLE DICK LEFT, DIDN'T IT?
YES. HE HAD ALWAYS THOUGHT-- AS I DID, I MUST ADMIT--THAT A DAY WOULD COME WHEN MASTER DICK WOULD TAKE OVER AS BATMAN!
AND I MIGHT YET, ALFRED!

UNCLE DICK!
MASTER DICK! YOU SHOULD HAVE LET US KNOW YOU WERE COMING!
AND RUIN THE SURPRISE?

BUT WHAT BRINGS YOU BACK, MASTER DICK? DARE WE HOPE...
NO... NOT QUITE READY TO BECOME BATMAN JUST YET, ALFRED. BRUCE STILL HAS A FEW ACTIVE YEARS IN HIM, I THINK!
BUT THINGS WERE SLOW IN THE D.A.'S OFFICE IN MANHATTAN, SO I THOUGHT I'D TAKE A FEW DAYS OFF TO VISIT. ER... WHERE IS BRUCE, BY THE WAY?
WE'RE NOT SURE, UNCLE DICK. DAD LEFT EARLY THIS MORNING AFTER A CALL FROM COMMISSIONER GORDON.

"WE HAVEN'T HEARD FROM HIM SINCE THEN."
MXYZPTLK PLAYS ROUGH!
AT LEAST BAT-MITE THINKS HE'S ON MY SIDE!

PART OF THE PROBLEM IS THAT MXY IS USED TO DEALING WITH SUPERMAN...
...SO HE KEEPS CONJURING THREATS THAT REQUIRE SUPER POWERS TO DEAL WITH THEM!
SINCE I DON'T HAVE SUPERMAN'S BAG OF TRICKS...
...I'LL HAVE TO IMPROVISE!
"HE'S NOT TOO MUCH FOR YOU, IS HE, MR. SUPERMAN?

I'M SURE BATMAN COULD FIND A WAY TO STOP THAT MONSTER!
BATMAN! OF COURSE!
AND IF MOHAMMED CAN'T COME TO THE MOUNTAIN...
HEY! WHAT ARE YOU DOING ??
...WELL TAKE THE MOUNTAIN TO MOHAMMED!
"I'VE MANAGED TO SLOW THE ROBOT--

BUT IT'S NOTHING MORE THAN A DE-LAYING TACTIC.
UNLESS I FIND A WAY TO STOP THE THING, HALF OF GOTHAM COULD BE WRECKED!
AND ON TOP OF THAT...
...TELL ME THAT ISN'T A TORNADO APPROACH ING!!
HEY!
BAT-MITE!
WHAT'S GOING ON HERE!?!
MY MONSTER IS FIGHTING YOUR MONSTER!
WE'LL HAVE TO FIND SOME OTHER WAY TO TEST OUR HEROES!

AND I KNOW JUST THE THING!
SPRANG INC
ANOTHER MONSTER!
SO NOW, IF GOTHAM DOESN'T GET CRUSHED, IT WILL GET BURNED TO THE GROUND!
MAYBE I CAN...
EH?
YES--YES, OF COURSE!
A BRILLIANT SOLUTION!
HEY! WHERE'S BATMAN GOING ..??
HE'S RUNNING AWAY!
HA HA HA HA! SO MUCH FOR YOUR BIG HERO, BAT-MITE!

NO! BATMAN, DON'T RUN! YOU'VE GOT TO FIND A WAY TO DEFEAT MXYZPTLK'S MONSTER!

BAT-MITE! NO!!

GOT YOU!

WAM

SUPERMAN! GET UP, YOU IDIOT! MY MONSTER WILL...
...CRUSH YOU...
≥GULP≤
IT...IT SQUASHED THEM BOTH!!
THOOM
THIS IS ALL YOUR FAULT, BAT-SPECK!
IF YOU HADN'T LET SUPERMAN BRING THAT PATHETIC MONSTER OF YOURS HERE...
MY PATHETIC MONSTER..?
I DON'T SEE HOW YOUR ROBOT WAS SO CLEVER, MXYZPTLK!
STOP!
THE ALIENS!
YOU HAVE PROVEN WHO ARE THE MOST POWERFUL AMONG YOU!

WE WILL TAKE THE TWO OF YOU BACK TO OUR PLANET!
WHEN YOU WHISPERED IN MY EAR VIA SUPER-VENTRILOQUISM, I KNEW IMMEDIATELY THAT YOUR PLAN WAS THE BEST WAY TO GET RID OF OUR LITTLE PESTS!!
YES--SINCE THE ALIENS WERE SO DETERMINED TO FIND THE MOST POWERFUL, WHO BETTER THAN BAT-MITE AND MXY TO FIT THEIR BILL!
IT WORKED!
IT DID GET A BIT HAIRY FOR A MOMENT THERE, THOUGH! IF YOU'D BEEN A FRACTION OF A SECOND OFF, TUNNELING DOWN AS THAT MONSTER STOMPED ON US...
SPLIT-SECOND TIMING IS EASY WITH MY POWERS, BATMAN. A LOT EASIER THAN IT'S GOING TO BE REPAIRING ALL THE DAMAGE DONE BY MXY AND BAT-MITE'S MONSTERS!
AH, WELL...
"AT LEAST FOR THE PRESENT THINGS ARE BACK TO NORMAL..."
JOEL KENT...
DON'T BE AFRAID, BOY. I HAVE SOMETHING IMPORTANT TO TELL YOU...
BUT... AREN'T YOU LEX LUTHOR..??

1969 Changing Times

WASHINGTON, D.C.--TWO YEARS AFTER THE SUMMER OF LOVE...

"WELL..??

CAN'T YOU DO SOME-THING ABOUT THIS?
WE COULD, MR. PRESIDENT.
BUT WE WON'T.
THOSE PEOPLE HAVE A CONSTITUTIONALLY-GUARANTEED RIGHT TO PROTEST.
THEY ARE OPPOSED TO THIS ASIAN WAR OF YOURS.

THEN WHY DON'T YOU DO SOME-THING ABOUT THAT?
GO OVER THERE AND END THAT WAR!
IT'S NOT THAT EASY, MR. PRESIDENT. THIS ISN'T WORLD WAR TWO. THE BAD GUYS ARE NOT SO CLEARLY DEFINED.

FINE! THEN JUST... LEAVE.
AND REMEMBER THAT EVERY AMERICAN BOY WHO DIES FROM TODAY ON WILL DIE BECAUSE YOU DID NOTHING TO PREVENT IT!
NOW, LOOK HERE...
LET IT GO, LANTERN. THERE'S NOTHING MORE WE CAN DO.

I WISH THERE WAS SOMETHING WE COULD DO. I WISH IT WAS MORE CLEAR-CUT...
YOU MORE THAN ANY OF US, CLARK. HAVE YOU HEARD FROM JOEL?
NOT IN NEARLY TWO WEEKS NOW. AND HIS PLATOON HAS BEEN MISSING FOR FIVE DAYS.
IF I COULD JUST FLY OVER THERE... I KNOW I COULD FIND THEM IN A MATTER OF MINUTES --IF THEY'RE STILL ALIVE.
BUT JOEL MADE YOU PROMISE YOU'D LET HIM DO HIS SERVICE ON HIS OWN.
HE HAS A LOT TO PROVE TO HIMSELF, BEING SUPERMAN'S SON.
YES... AND I STILL HAVE NO IDEA WHEN AND HOW HE FOUND OUT. LOIS AND I WERE SO CAREFUL... BUT IT'S BEEN AL-MOST TEN YEARS...
ENOUGH ABOUT MY TROUBLES, THOUGH. WHAT ABOUT BRUCE JR.? IS HE STILL INSIST-ING ON SERV-ING?
YES. HE SAYS HE DOESN'T SEE HOW IT WOULD BE RIGHT TO LET BRUCE USE HIS INFLUENCE TO KEEP HIM OUT OF THE DRAFT.
ANOTHER WEEK, AND HE'LL BE LEAVING FOR BASIC TRAINING. AND I'LL BECOME THE SECOND BATMAN TO LOSE HIS ROBIN!
"THERE'S NOTHING I CAN DO, OLD FRIEND.
AND--THERE'S NOTHING I SHOULD DO. MY SON IS RIGHT. HE MUST FOLLOW THE DICTATES OF HIS OWN CONSCIENCE!
ALFRED THADDEUS CRANE PENNYWORTH
1889-1967
"NO FRIEND MORE FAITHFUL."
AS YOU HAVE ALWAYS DONE, SIR.

THERE YOU ARE. I WAS BEGINNING TO THINK YOU MIGHT NOT COME, THIS TIME.
YOU KNOW I WILL AL-WAYS BE HERE WHEN YOU NEED ME, SIR.

AND YOU'LL NEVER CALL ME ANYTHING BUT "SIR" OR "MASTER BRUCE," WILL YOU, ALFRED? NEVER JUST "BRUCE."
BUT THEN, THE ALFRED I REMEMBER WOULD NEVER DO SUCH A THING, WOULD HE?
AND YOU ARE STILL CONVINCED THAT IS WHAT I AM--YOUR MEMORIES OF ME?

I DON'T THINK ABOUT IT AS MUCH AS I USED TO, OLD FRIEND.
IT'S ENOUGH THAT YOU COME WHEN I NEED YOU--AND YOU ALWAYS SAY WHAT I NEED TO HEAR.
NOT ALWAYS. YOU WERE QUITE RE-SISTANT WHEN I SAID THE TIME HAD COME FOR YOU TO PASS ON THE CAPE AND COWL OF THE BATMAN.

"THE" BATMAN. YOU'RE THE ONLY ONE WHO STILL USES THE DEFINITE ARTICLE, ALFRED.
MY FAULT, I GUESS. A FEW TOO MANY CHARITY BALLS AND LIBRARY OPENINGS. PEOPLE GOT USED TO SEEING BATMAN. THEY FORGOT TO BE SCARED OF HIM...
MORE THAN ENOUGH IN THE WORLD FOR THEM TO BE SCARED OF, MASTER BRUCE.
WHAT THE PEOPLE NEED NOW, MORE THAN EVER, IS A ROCK THEY CAN DEPEND ON. WHICH IS WHY THEY NEEDED A YOUNG AND VIGOROUS BATMAN.

YES--YOU WERE ABSOLUTELY RIGHT ABOUT THAT. AND DICK WAS RIGHT TO TRY TO CONVINCE PEOPLE HE'S THE SAME BATMAN.
CONTINUITY IS IMPORTANT. A SENSE OF HISTORY AND TRADITION.
QUITE SO, SIR.
BUT, WHEN DOES YOUNG MASTER BRUCE LEAVE, NOW?
IN TWO DAYS. HE AND DICK ARE OUT ON WHAT'S LIKELY TO BE HIS LAST CASE AS ROBIN, RIGHT NOW.
AND I NEED TO GET BACK TO THE BATCAVE, IN CASE THEY CALL IN. THANKS AGAIN, ALFRED.
ALWAYS MY PLEASURE, SIR.
AND... IF YOU WOULD--TRY TO THINK OF ME LESS AS A HALLUCINATION...
"...AND MORE AS A FAITHFUL FAMILY RETAINER, WHO WILL NOT LEAVE UNTIL HE KNOWS HIS TASK IS TRULY DONE."
HE'S NO SON OF MINE, NO MATTER WHAT HE SAYS!
UNLIKE YOU, I NEVER HAD TIME FOR OFFSPRING.
YET HE HAS ALL YOUR TRICKS DOWN PAT, JOKER. IF YOU DIDN'T SIRE HIM, I'D BET GOOD MONEY YOU TRAINED HIM.
TRAINED HIM WELL ENOUGH TO HAVE SUCCESSFULLY ELUDED CAPTURE FOR ALMOST FOUR YEARS NOW!

TALKING TO THE JOKER WAS A LAST DITCH EFFORT. I'M NOT SURE WHAT I EXPECTED TO LEARN.

I WAS HALFWAY CONVINCED WE'D FIND HIM GONE... THAT HE'D BUSTED OUT AND WAS COACHING JOKER JUNIOR.

AND, YOU KNOW... THE THING THAT GALLS ME THE MOST IS BEING CONSTANTLY HOODWINKED BY SOMEONE WITH SUCH A GOOFY NAME!

PART OF HIS PSYCHOLOGY, I THINK, BRUCE.

A LITTLE SOMETHING TO KEEP US CONSTANTLY UNDERESTIMATING HIM!

"I'M SORRY, MRS. KENT... I'M AFRAID THERE CAN BE NO DOUBT."

CANCER? OF COURSE. HOW LONG HAVE I GOT?
NOW, NOW, MRS. KENT--THERE'S REALLY NO REASON TO TAKE SUCH A GLOOMY ATTITUDE. WITH THE MEDICAL ADVANCES WE HAVE TODAY...

...I CAN PROLONG MY SUFFERING FOR YEARS!
I'M SERIOUS, DOCTOR. HOW LONG?
EVERY CASE VARIES. THERE'S NO WAY TO BE SURE. IT COULD BE YEARS, WITH THERAPY, WITH POTENTIAL REMISSION...

AND IT COULD BE MONTHS, OR EVEN WEEKS, RIGHT?
OKAY--TIME TO GET MY HOUSE IN ORDER. THANK YOU, DOCTOR.
YOU SAY THAT AS IF WE WON'T BE SEEING EACH OTHER AGAIN, MRS. KENT.

WE PROBABLY WON'T, DOCTOR.
MOM ..?
WHEN SHALL I SCHEDULE ANOTHER APPOINTMENT, MRS. KENT?

YOU WON'T, MARGARET.
COME ON, KARA, HONEY. I NEED A RIDE HOME...

MOM, I COULDN'T HELP OVER-HEARING...
OF COURSE NOT. YOU MAY HAVE ONLY HALF YOUR FATHER'S POWERS AND ABILITIES, BUT THAT STILL PUTS YOU FAR ABOVE THOSE OF MORTAL MEN--OR WOMEN.
I'VE GOTTEN USED TO HAVING NO SECRETS FROM YOU.

YOU'RE NOT REALLY GOING TO GIVE UP, ARE YOU, MOM?
DAD AND I COULD SCOUR THE UNIVERSE FOR A CURE...
NO--YOUR FATHER TRIED THAT YEARS AGO. HE FOUND A HUNDRED WORLDS WITH CURES FOR A MILLION DISEASES...
NONE OF WHICH WORKED ON HUMAN PHYSIOLOGY. JUST LIKE HE WAS NEVER ABLE TO FIND A SERUM THAT WOULD GIVE JOEL AND ME THE SAME POWERS YOU AND CLARK HAVE.
BUT... MOM... YOU CAN'T JUST--JUST...
DIE? SURE I CAN, HONEY. EVERYTHING DOES, AFTER ALL. AND--LET'S FACE IT! I SHOULD HAVE LEARNED A BIG LESSON WHEN THOSE CIGARS FINALLY KILLED YOUR UNCLE PERRY.
NOW--PLEASE, SWEETIE... I DON'T WANT TO TALK ABOUT IT.

"I JUST WANT TO GO HOME..."
WHERE THE HELL IS HE? AND WHERE THE HELL ARE WE??

IN DEEP TROUBLE IS WHERE WE ARE, DOOLEY.
WE CROSSED THE BORDER MORE'N EIGHTEEN HOURS AGO.
BUT... BUT THE LIEUTENANT SAYS WE DIDN'T, ROGERS. HE SAYS WE'RE STILL ON THE 'NAM SIDE.
LIKE HE'S GONNA SAY ANYTHING ELSE?
YEAH--WELL, WHEREVER WE ARE, KENT'S BEEN GONE FOR OVER AN HOUR NOW. EITHER HE DIDN'T FIND WHAT HE WAS LOOKING FOR...
OR IT FOUND HIM!
LOOK--WE CAN BE BACK ACROSS THE BORDER AGAIN IN LESS THAN TWELVE HOURS IF WE GO NON-STOP. I VOTE WE TURN BACK.
I'LL TAKE THAT UNDER CONSIDER-ATION, SMITH...
...THE MOMENT THE ARMY BECOMES A DEMOC-RACY.
LIEUTEN-ANT KENT! MAN, ARE WE GLAD TO SEE YOU!
SPEAK FOR YOUR SELF, CARTER... LOOK. SIR, WE'RE WAY OFF OUR PATROL AND WAY OUTTA LINE HERE. IF CHARLIE CATCHES US, IT'LL BE LIKE WE JUST FELL OFF THE PLANET!

ROGERS IS BEIN' A BIT BLUNT, SIR, BUT HE'S SAYIN' WHAT WE'RE ALL THINKING.
I DON'T KNOW WHY YOU BROUGHT US ACROSS THE BORDER, BUT WE GOTTA GO BACK!
BACK? WITH A CONG BASE JUST THE OTHER SIDE OF THAT RIDGE?
MAYBE YOU'VE FORGOTTEN WHAT WE'RE HERE FOR, CORPORAL.
NO ONE'S FORGOT ANYTHING ...BUT OUR JOB ISN'T TO HUNT CHARLIE ANYWHERE OUTSIDE TH' 'NAM.

THAT'S WHERE YOU'RE WRONG, JACKSON. OUR JOB IS TO FIND AND KILL THE ENEMY. AND IF WE TAKE OUT THAT BASE, WE'LL DO THAT...

"AND SAVE THOUSANDS OF AMERICAN LIVES IN THE PROCESS."
THAT'S A CONG BASE??
IT'S A LOUSY VILLAGE! NOTHIN' BUT WOMEN AN' KIDS AN' OLD MEN!
WHAT DID YOU EXPECT, JACKSON? A RED CHINESE FLAG? PORTRAITS OF HO CHI MINH? THE CONG ARE HERE--AND IF WE DELAY ANY LONGER, THEY'LL KNOW WE'RE HERE!
"NOW, LET'S DO WHAT WE CAME HERE TO DO!"
THAT'S ALL OF THEM, LIEUTENANT--ALL THE SURVIVORS.
WHERE ARE THE REST? WHERE ARE THE YOUNG MEN?
THERE AREN'T ANY, SIR! NO MEN AT ALL, EXCEPT THIS OLD GUY!

THEN HE'LL HAVE TO TELL US WHERE THE OTHERS ARE HIDING, BEFORE THEY CAN AMBUSH US.
WELL, OLD MAN? WHERE ARE THEY? WHERE ARE THE CONG FIGHTERS?
I SAID WHERE??
GEEZ, SIR! TAKE IT EASY! HE'S JUST AN OLD MAN!
HANDS OFF, CARTER. OR HAVE YOU DECIDED TO TURN ON ME LIKE THE REST OF THESE COWARDS?
NOBODY'S TURNING ON NOBODY, LIEUTENANT --BUT YOU WERE WRONG ABOUT THIS VILLAGE...
...AND NOW WE BETTER GET OUT OF HERE BE - FORE SOMEBODY FINDS OUT WE SLAUGHTERED NONCOMBATANTS!
YOU'VE BEEN SMOKING TOO MUCH OF THE LOCAL FLORA, JACKSON.
THERE'S NO SUCH THING AS A NONCOMBATANT ON THE OTHER SIDE IN THIS WAR.
BUT YOU'RE RIGHT ABOUT ONE THING.
WE CAN'T LEAVE THESE ALIVE TO REPORT TO THEIR COMMIE MASTERS.
S-SIR? WHAT ARE YOU GOING TO DO..??
HE'S NOT GONNA DO NOTHIN', CARTER. HE'S ALREADY DONE TOO MUCH!
"IT SEEMS LIKE THE ONLY WAY I CAN CRACK THIS CASE IS BY BEING IN TWO PLACES AT ONCE!"

WELL,--WHY NOT, THEN? I'VE GOT THIS COLLAPSIBLE BAT-SUIT IN MY UTILITY BELT.
MAYBE THIS IS THE EMERGENCY WE WERE THINKING OF WHEN WE ASKED BARRY ALLEN TO HELP US CREATE IT!
AND YOU KNOW I'VE GOT THE BAT-VOICE DOWN PAT!
YES--PERFECT... BUT WE CAN'T AFFORD TO HAVE BATMAN SEEN IN MORE THAN ONE PLACE AT A TIME.
NO--THAT WOULD DESTROY THE ILLUSION THAT I'M THE ORIGINAL BATMAN. AND EVEN THE JOKER SEEMS TO BELIEVE THAT!
ARNING!
IDNITE I
LL PAY A VISIT
ON A MULTI-FACETED
OLD LADY OF A
RECENT FACE-LIFT
JOKER JUNIOR!
JOKER... HE'S DEFINITELY UP TO SOMETHING. YOU'RE NOT THE ONLY ONE WHOSE SIXTH SENSE HAS BEEN TINGLING, DICK.
BUT A DIVISION OF FORCES SEEMS LIKE THE ONLY ANSWER.
ROBIN--YOU GO BACK TO ROCK ISLAND AND SEE WHAT YOU CAN SHAKE OUT OF THE JOKER'S TREE...

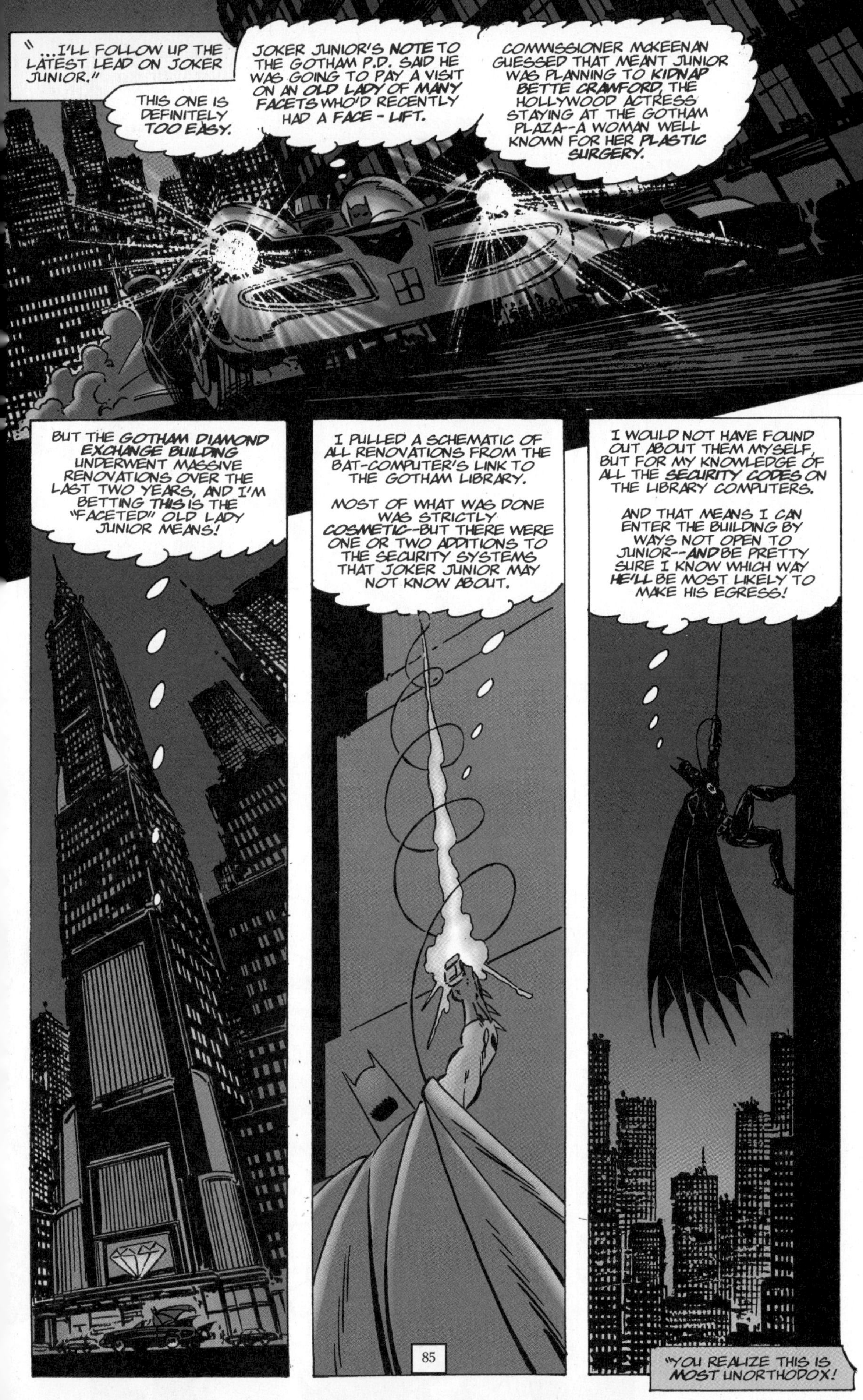
"...I'LL FOLLOW UP THE LATEST LEAD ON JOKER JUNIOR."
THIS ONE IS DEFINITELY TOO EASY.
JOKER JUNIOR'S NOTE TO THE GOTHAM P.D. SAID HE WAS GOING TO PAY A VISIT ON AN OLD LADY OF MANY FACETS WHO'D RECENTLY HAD A FACE - LIFT.
COMMISSIONER McKEENAN GUESSED THAT MEANT JUNIOR WAS PLANNING TO KIDNAP BETTE CRAWFORD, THE HOLLYWOOD ACTRESS STAYING AT THE GOTHAM PLAZA--A WOMAN WELL KNOWN FOR HER PLASTIC SURGERY.
BUT THE GOTHAM DIAMOND EXCHANGE BUILDING UNDERWENT MASSIVE RENOVATIONS OVER THE LAST TWO YEARS, AND I'M BETTING THIS IS THE "FACETED" OLD LADY JUNIOR MEANS!
I PULLED A SCHEMATIC OF ALL RENOVATIONS FROM THE BAT-COMPUTER'S LINK TO THE GOTHAM LIBRARY.
MOST OF WHAT WAS DONE WAS STRICTLY COSMETIC--BUT THERE WERE ONE OR TWO ADDITIONS TO THE SECURITY SYSTEMS THAT JOKER JUNIOR MAY NOT KNOW ABOUT.
I WOULD NOT HAVE FOUND OUT ABOUT THEM MYSELF, BUT FOR MY KNOWLEDGE OF ALL THE SECURITY CODES ON THE LIBRARY COMPUTERS.
AND THAT MEANS I CAN ENTER THE BUILDING BY WAYS NOT OPEN TO JUNIOR--AND BE PRETTY SURE I KNOW WHICH WAY HE'LL BE MOST LIKELY TO MAKE HIS EGRESS!
"YOU REALIZE THIS IS MOST UNORTHODOX!

WE PREFER NOT TO HAVE THE PRISONERS DISTURBED AFTER LOCK-DOWN.
I APPRECIATE THAT, WARDEN CHARLES.
BUT IT'S ABSOLUTELY VITAL WE CHECK ON THE JOKER RIGHT NOW.
WELL--THERE, YOU SEE--THE JOKER IS STILL SAFE AND SOUND IN HIS CELL!
I ASSURE YOU, ROBIN, THERE IS NO WAY HE COULD HAVE ESCAPED FROM THIS MAXIMUM SECURITY WING. IN THE HUNDRED YEARS THIS PRISON HAS BEEN IN SERVICE, NO ONE EVER HAS!
THAT WAS A CENTURY WITHOUT HAVING TO DEAL WITH THE JOKER. SIR.
OPEN THE CELL, PLEASE...
VERY WELL--BUT I SHOULD WARN YOU I INTEND TO LODGE A FORMAL PROTEST WITH COMMISSIONER McKEENAN AS SOON AS HIS OFFICE OPENS IN THE MORNING!
WARDEN --IN ALL HONESTY, I HOPE YOU'LL HAVE A REASON TO LODGE THAT PROTEST!
BUT IT DOESN'T LOOK LIKE YOU WILL!
OH, MY!
HEY! WHAT'S THAT?

DON'T TOUCH IT! IT COULD BE A BOOBY-TRAP!
THERE'S SOME KIND OF SHELF UNDER THE TABLE--LOOKS LIKE JOKER HAS A LITTLE HIDING PLACE HERE...
HIS PRISON UNIFORM--JARS OF THEATRICAL MAKE-UP--INCLUDING SPIRIT GUM FOR ATTACHING A FAKE BEARD OR WIG.
AND WHAT'S THIS...?
LOOKS LIKE...A BLUEPRINT?
THAT'S JUST WHAT IT IS--A BLUEPRINT OF THE DIAMOND EXCHANGE BUILDING.
BUT THIS SHOWS ALL KINDS OF STUFF THAT WASN'T ON THE PLANS BATMAN ACQUIRED.
STUFF THAT MEANS BATMAN IS IN DEADLY DANGER!!
BUT... BUT...

"WHAT ABOUT THE JOKER??"
LOOKS LIKE I'M EARLY. NO SIGN THAT JOKER JUNIOR HAS MADE HIS MOVE YET.
WITH THESE INFRARED GOGGLES, I CAN SEE ALL THE SECURITY BEAMS CRISSCROSSING THE ROOM.
THEY SPIN AN IMPENETRABLE WEB AROUND THE CENTERPIECE OF THIS EXHIBIT--AND THE STONE THAT IS ALMOST CERTAIN TO BE JUNIOR'S TARGET.
NOW, ALL I NEED TO DO IS CONCEAL MYSELF IN THE SPOT I PREVIOUSLY SELECTED, AND...
THE FLOOR !!
SOME KIND OF TRAP DOOR!
IT WASN'T ON THE PLANS--BUT THIS SHAFT IS NARROW ENOUGH FOR ME TO BRACE MYSELF AGAINST THE WALLS...

AH-GH!!
RAZOR-SHARP BLADES!
I CAN'T HOLD ON!!
SHAFT--GETTING NARROWER!
BLADES ARE CUTTING ME TO RIBBONS!
UNGH!
THAT... SLOWED...WHAT WOULD...HAVE BEEN A..FATAL FALL...
BUT--BLEEDING... HEAVILY. SOME OF THOSE CUTS WENT... ALL THE WAY...TO THE BONE!
YOU MIGHT SAY I... BONED UP ON YOUR WEAKNESSES, EH, BATSY?
JUNIOR!
MY... CONGRATULATIONS! IT MUST HAVE TAKEN... YEARS TO SET UP... THIS SCHEME!
ALMOST TEN YEARS, BATMAN.
BEGINNING WITH USING MY ILL-GOTTEN GAINS TO CREATE A DUMMY CORPORATION TO PURCHASE THE DIAMOND EXCHANGE BUILDING.

TEN YEARS? BUT THAT'S SIX YEARS LONGER THAN "JOKER JUNIOR" HAS BEEN AROUND... AT LEAST, LONGER THAN YOU'VE BEEN OPERATING IN GOTHAM.
DON'T STRAIN YOUR BRAIN, BAT-BOOB. IT'S GOING TO GET HARD ENOUGH TO WORK THAT PARTICULAR ORGAN AS IT IS! AFTER ALL--I COATED THOSE BLADES WITH A NEAT LITTLE COCKTAIL OF HALLUCINOGENIC DRUGS.
WHICH SHOULD BE KICK-ING IN RIGHT ABOUT... NOW.
IT'LL TAKE...MORE...THAN THAT TO STOP ME, JOKER...
THINK SO?
THE LOSS OF BLOOD ALONE WOULD BE ENOUGH TO MAKE YOU WOOZY.
ADD THAT TO ALL THE GOODIES I'VE PREPARED FOR YOU HERE--AND I DON'T THINK YOUR ARROGANCE IS GONNA DO YOU MUCH GOOD!
FLOOR... TIPPING...
OR...IS IT...THE DRUGS ..?

WHAT... IN..??
GIANT PIES..??
COULDN'T LET OUR LAST ENCOUNTER PASS WITHOUT A FEW OVERSIZED PROPS, NOW COULD I, BAT-CHUMP?
MERINGUE... ATTACKING ME..!!
THAT'S THE WAY, BATTY!
I HAVE NO IDEA WHAT YOU THINK YOU'RE SEEING...
"...BUT I'LL BET MY BEST GAG IT HAS NOTHING TO DO WITH THE REAL THREAT!"
WHAT ARE YOU STANDING AROUND OUT HERE FOR?
WHEN I RADIOED IN, I TOLD YOU BATMAN WAS IN DANGER!
WE KNOW, ROBIN! BUT ALL THE SECURITY CODES HAVE BEEN CHANGED!
WE CAN'T GET INTO THE BUILDING!
OMIGOSH! LISTEN!!
GPD

MACHINE GUN FIRE!
ACCORDING TO THE PLANS IN JOKER'S CELL, THAT'S THE LAST TRAP!
IF THAT TRAP HAS BEEN SPRUNG...
NO! NO! I MUSTN'T THINK THAT WAY!
NO MATTER WHAT THE JOKER DID, BATMAN WOULD FIND A WAY TO...
BATMAN ..!!!

SPREAD OUT! AND BE CAREFUL!
NO TELLING WHAT TRAPS JOKER JUNIOR HAS LAID!
NONE FOR YOU, BOYS IN BLUE!
PUT AWAY THE POP GUNS, CHILDREN! I'LL COME QUIETLY! I'VE ACCOMPLISHED MY LIFE'S AMBITION!
WH-WHAT ARE YOU TALKING ABOUT, JUNIOR?
NO MORE "JUNIOR," IF YOU DON'T MIND!
I WASN'T LYING WHEN I TOLD BATMAN I'D NEVER HAD A SON OR TRAINED A PROTÉGÉ.
I AM THE JOKER! AND I AM THE MAN WHO JUST KILLED BATMAN!!
SUCH A WONDERFULLY SIMPLE PLAN IT WAS, TOO! ONCE I DISCOVERED HOW EASY IT WAS TO GET OFF AND ON ROCK ISLAND.
WHAT BETTER HIDING PLACE FOR A WANTED CRIMINAL THAN IN PRISON!
Y-YOU R-REALLY KILLED BATMAN ..??
NO--AS USUAL HE'S LYING.

HE DIDN'T KILL BATMAN.
HE KILLED ROBIN!

Epilogue

IT'S NOT AT ALL THE WAY I ENVISIONED THIS SCENE, MASTER BRUCE.

SOMEHOW, I ALWAYS KNEW I'D BE STANDING ON THIS HILLSIDE WITH YOU, WATCHING A WARRIOR BEING LAID TO REST...

...BUT YOU THOUGHT THAT WARRIOR WOULD BE ME, AND THAT I'D BE A... GHOST, LIKE YOU.

WHAT ABOUT DICK, ALFRED? IS HE... ALL RIGHT?

I'M AFRAID I CANNOT SAY, SIR. MASTER DICK'S SPIRIT HAS GONE TO A PLACE... OTHER THAN THE ONE FAMILIAR TO ME.

BUT, AFTER A LIFE SO FULL OF COURAGE AND COMPASSION...

"I GUESS I'LL HAVE TO LET YOU USE YOUR INFLUENCE TO GET ME THAT ABEYANCE AFTER ALL, DAD...!"

DON'T BE SAD, KARA. B.J. LOVES YOU. I CAN TELL BY THE LOOK IN HIS EYES.

FINISH COLLEGE, LIKE YOU PLANNED, AND BY THEN...

...MAYBE THE WORLD WILL BE READY FOR A BATMAN AND SUPERGIRL TEAM?

YOU'RE RIGHT, MOM. BUT THEN...

"...YOU USUALLY ARE!"

WHY DON'T YOU LIE DOWN FOR A WHILE, HONEY? YOU SEEM... TIRED...

OH--LOOK. SOMEONE SLIPPED A TELEGRAM THROUGH THE LETTER BOX.

MAYBE IT'S FINALLY SOME GOOD NEWS ABOUT JOEL...

OH... NO!

OH NO! NO! NO!!

TO: MR. & MRS. CLARK KENT
27 WILTON AVE. METROPOLIS
FROM: WAR DEPARTMENT, WASHINGTON DC
SEPT. 22 1969

IT IS WITH GREAT REGRET THAT WE INFORM YOU YOUR SON JOEL PERRY KENT WAS REPORTED KILLED IN ACTION SEPT. 13 1969.

MORRISON A. RUTHERFORD
GEN. OF THE ARMY.

1979
Twilight of the Gods

Miss Kent And Mr. Wayne

Kara Kent and Bruce Wayne Jr. will be married at Wayne Manor in Gotham City. The Rev. Percival Dennis of Metropolis will perform the ceremony.

Miss Kent is a televison remporter with the Galaxy WorldWide Network. The bride, 26, graduated from Metropolis University. She is a daughter of Lois and Clark Kent of Metropolis. Her father is Editor-in-Chief of the Metropilis *Daily Planet*. Her mother is a retired reporter for that paper.

Mr. Wayne, 29, is president and CEO of Wayne Industries. He graduated from Cambridge and received degrees in science, law and psychology at Gotham University. He is [illegible] and Bruce Wayne of Gotham City. His father retired as the president of Wayne Industries and remains as head of the Wayne Foundation. The bridegroom's mother is a dealer in international antiquities.

Miss Began Mr. Chan

Courtney Lamb Began, a daughter of Rebbeca and Walter Began of Gotham City is to be married to Alexander Gabriel Chan, the son of Cheryl and James Chan of Philadelphia. The Reverend Barry Conni... will perform the ceremony at the First Congregational Church ... Gotham City.

Miss Began, 27, is a freela... graphic designer. She gradu... from Skidmore College. Her fa... is a senior partner at Mad... Rausch and Killin, the manage... consulting concern in New Yo...

Mr. Chan, also 27, is an a... supervisor at Valdez and K... promotion and marketing co... in Morristown, NJ. He g... from the University of ... His father is a managemen... tant in Philadelphia.

DON'T AGITATE YOURSELF, HONEY. YOU KNOW WHAT THE DOCTORS SAID...
I KNOW--BUT I'VE BEEN A REPORTER FOR ALMOST FIFTY YEARS...
...AND THE UNION OF THE TWO GREATEST SUPER-HERO FAMILIES IS A STORY TOO GOOD TO MISS!
BE GLAD PEOPLE ARE "MISSING" THAT ELEMENT, LOIS. THERE HAVE BEEN ENOUGH QUESTIONS ABOUT WHY THE SON OF THE FOURTH RICHEST MAN IN AMERICA WOULD BE MARRYING THE DAUGHTER OF A COUPLE OF LOWLY NEWSPAPER REPORTERS!
I KNOW... I KNOW.
AS A MOTHER I SHOULD JUST BE PLEASED KARA FOUND SOMEONE AS WONDERFUL AS B.J.!
LAST TIME I SAW HIM, HE WAS PREFERRING "BRUCE" AGAIN. MORE IN KEEPING WITH HIS ROLE AS THE HEAD OF THE WAYNE FOUNDATION.
FUNNY--WHEN YOU AND I FIRST MET HIS FATHER, HALF A CENTURY AGO, WE NEVER COULD HAVE PREDICTED...
SORRY TO INTRUDE...
MR. AND MRS. KENT? I'M DOCTOR HOLURT.
THE SPECIALIST DR. MAXWELL TOLD US ABOUT? GLAD YOU COULD COME ON SUCH SHORT NOTICE, DOCTOR.
YES--MAXWELL THINKS YOU MAY ACTUALLY BE ABLE TO KEEP ME ALIVE UNTIL THE WEDDING!
OH, LONGER THAN THAT I SHOULD THINK, MRS. KENT.
I WONDER--MR. KENT, WOULD YOU MIND IF I HAVE A FEW MINUTES ALONE WITH YOUR GOOD LADY WIFE?
NO, THAT'LL BE FINE, DOCTOR. I HAVE TO GET BACK TO THE PLANET, ANYWAY.

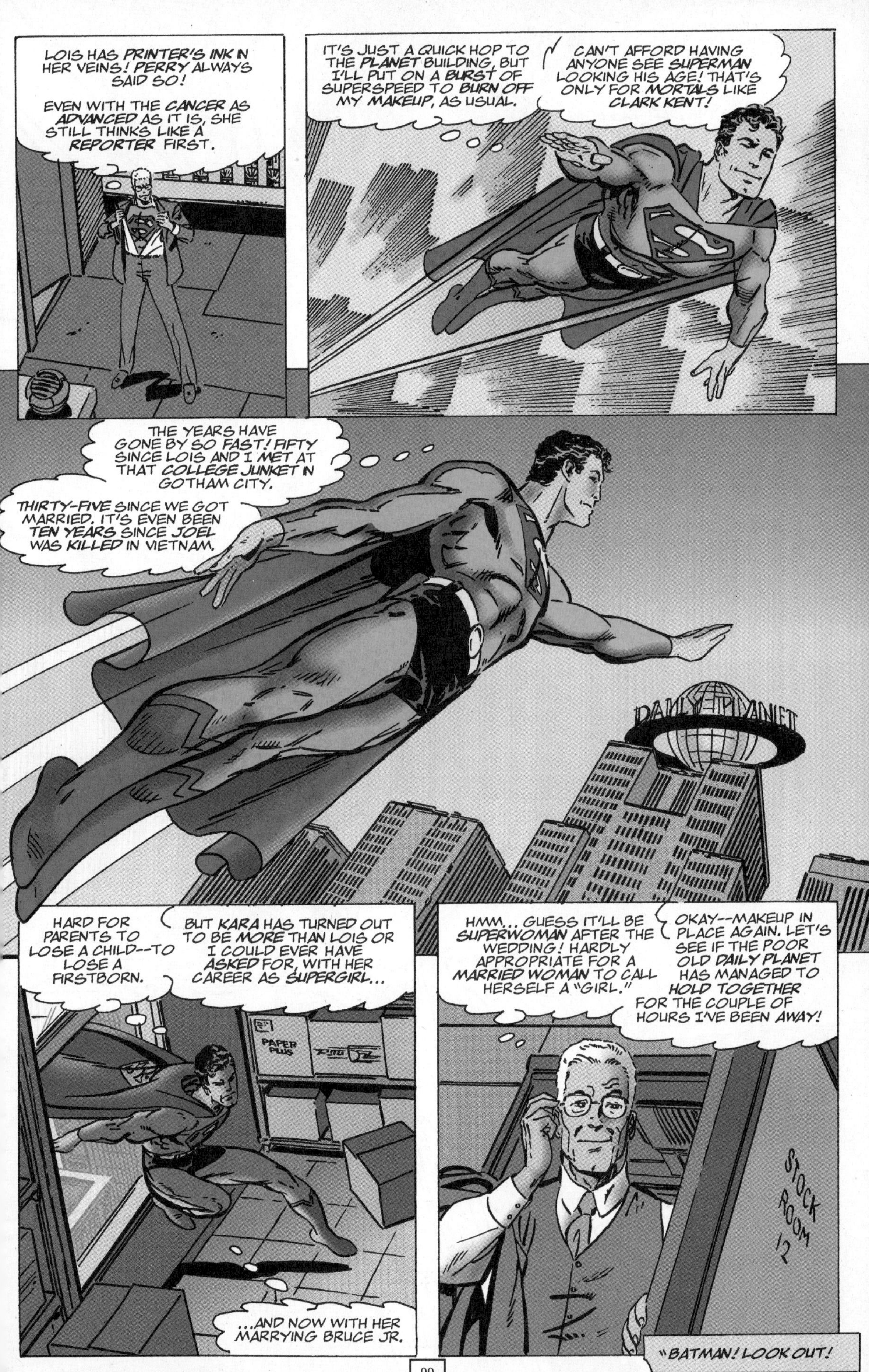
LOIS HAS PRINTER'S INK IN HER VEINS! PERRY ALWAYS SAID SO!
EVEN WITH THE CANCER AS ADVANCED AS IT IS, SHE STILL THINKS LIKE A REPORTER FIRST.
IT'S JUST A QUICK HOP TO THE PLANET BUILDING, BUT I'LL PUT ON A BURST OF SUPERSPEED TO BURN OFF MY MAKEUP, AS USUAL.
CAN'T AFFORD HAVING ANYONE SEE SUPERMAN LOOKING HIS AGE! THAT'S ONLY FOR MORTALS LIKE CLARK KENT!
THE YEARS HAVE GONE BY SO FAST! FIFTY SINCE LOIS AND I MET AT THAT COLLEGE JUNKET IN GOTHAM CITY.
THIRTY-FIVE SINCE WE GOT MARRIED. IT'S EVEN BEEN TEN YEARS SINCE JOEL WAS KILLED IN VIETNAM.
DAILY PLANET
HARD FOR PARENTS TO LOSE A CHILD--TO LOSE A FIRSTBORN.
BUT KARA HAS TURNED OUT TO BE MORE THAN LOIS OR I COULD EVER HAVE ASKED FOR, WITH HER CAREER AS SUPERGIRL...
PAPER PLUS
...AND NOW WITH HER MARRYING BRUCE JR.
HMM... GUESS IT'LL BE SUPERWOMAN AFTER THE WEDDING! HARDLY APPROPRIATE FOR A MARRIED WOMAN TO CALL HERSELF A "GIRL."
OKAY--MAKEUP IN PLACE AGAIN. LET'S SEE IF THE POOR OLD DAILY PLANET HAS MANAGED TO HOLD TOGETHER FOR THE COUPLE OF HOURS I'VE BEEN AWAY!
STOCK ROOM 12
"BATMAN! LOOK OUT!

LOOKS LIKE BRAINIAC'S HUNTER-KILLER MISSILES HAVE WORKED THEIR WAY THROUGH YOUR JAMMING FREQUENCY!
WE'LL HAVE TO GO BACK TO THE OLD-FASHIONED METHODS OF DEALING WITH 'EM!
JUST HOLD THEM OFF FOR A FEW MORE SECONDS, SWEET-HEART!
I'M ALMOST DONE HERE!

THERE! I'VE CROSS-CIRCUITED ALL THE MAIN CONTROL SYSTEMS.
BRAINIAC WILL STILL BE ABLE TO NAVIGATE HIS SHIP OUT OF OUR SOLAR SYSTEM...
BUT IF HE TRIES ANYTHING ELSE, HE'S GONNA BE ONE SORRY COMPUTER!
FOOLISH HUMANS!
DO YOU TRULY BELIEVE MY PLANS CAN BE UNDONE BY YOUR PATHETIC ORGANIC BRAINS?
NOTHING CAN STOP MY ANNIHILATION OF THE PLANET EARTH!
AND IN A FEW MOMENTS, WHEN MY MECHA-MORPHOSIS IS COMPLETED, I SHALL BE READY TO CARRY A SIMILAR FATE TO EVERY INHABITED WORLD IN THE GALAXY!
HE MEANS IT! I'VE GOT TO FIND HIM!
KARA! NO! THAT COULD TAKE DAYS IN THE LABYRINTHIAN CORRIDORS OF THIS SHIP.

"WE'VE GOT TO GET CLEAR BEFORE HE ATTEMPTS TO ACTIVATE ANY OF HIS ONBOARD SYSTEMS!"
KARA! USE YOUR SUPER-STRENGTH TO PUSH BRAINIAC'S SHIP OUT OF EARTH ORBIT!
THE EFFECT OF MY TINKERING MAY BE... DRAMATIC!
WILL DO!
UNH!! DAD COULD DO THIS WITH ONE HAND, WITHOUT EVEN WORKING UP A SWEAT. BUT I ONLY HAVE HALF HIS POWER LEVELS!
STILL--AS BRUCE SAID, ONCE UPON A TIME, HALF OF INFINITY IS STILL INFINITY!
THERE IT GOES! BUT MY X-RAY VISION SHOWS ALL KINDS OF CIRCUITRY COMING TO LIFE!
BRAINIAC IS LAUNCHING HIS ATTACK...

GREAT KRYPTON!!
IT'S COLLAPSING!

THE WHOLE SHIP IS CRUSHING ITSELF INTO A BLACK HOLE!

AND THE PULL OF THE MASSIVE GRAVITY IS SUCKING BATMAN'S SHIP RIGHT INTO THE COLLAPSE!

HANG ON, HONEY!
HAVING YOU COMPRESSED TO SUBATOMIC SIZE WOULD REALLY WRECK OUR WEDDING PLANS!
JUST A FEW MOMENTS LONGER, KARA!
ACCORDING TO MY SCANNERS, BRAINIAC'S SHIP IS AT COMPRESSION THRESHOLD...

"THERE IT GOES!!"
WOW! WHAT THE HECK WAS THAT?
ACCORDING TO MY TELESCOPIC VISION, THAT WAS MY DAUGHTER AND SOON-TO-BE SON-IN-LAW TAKING CARE OF BUSINESS AS USUAL!
SOMETHING WE'LL FIND OUT ABOUT SOON ENOUGH I'M SURE, JIM.
NOW, WHAT'S THIS ABOUT YOU RETIRING?

SPEAKING OF WHICH--I HAVE A COLUMN TO GET FINISHED FOR TODAY'S PAPER, OR MY EDITOR-IN-CHIEF WILL BE ALL OVER ME!

YOU KNOW WHAT A TYRANT HE IS!

EDITOR IN CHIEF

CLARK KENT

YES! I UNDERSTAND HE'S A REAL BEAR!

EXTRAORDINARY! I NEVER THOUGHT I'D SEE THE DAY JIMMY OLSEN WOULD LEAVE THE DAILY PLANET OF HIS OWN ACCORD!

IT SEEMS AS THOUGH MY LIFE IS TAKING ON A WHOLE PATTERN OF ENDINGS LATELY. AT LEAST I HAVE KARA'S WEDDING TO LOOK FORWARD TO. THAT IS A BRIGHT AND SHINING BEGINNING.

"JUST A FEW MORE INCHES...

COME ON, WAYNE! YOU CAN DO IT! YOU'RE ONLY AS OLD AS YOU FEEL!
BUT--HUHN--UNFORTUNATELY ... RIGHT NOW... I FEEL...ABOUT A THOUSAND... YEARS OLD.
KEEP... GOING. ALMOST...THERE...NOW. IF I STOP...NOW...I'LL NEVER...GET UP...AGAIN...
GOT... TO...
"WELCOME, ADVERSARY.

THIS MEETING HAS BEEN POSTPONED TOO LONG.
WHERE...?
YOU! THEN I WAS RIGHT! THE LEGENDS ARE TRUE!
INDEED THEY ARE, ADVERSARY.
I AM RA'S AL GHUL, AND THIS IS MY DAUGHTER, TALIA. WE HAVE BEEN ANTICIPATING YOUR ARRIVAL FOR SOME TIME, NOW.
I'D HAVE BEEN HERE A LOT SOONER, IF I COULD. I'D HAVE STOPPED YOU YEARS AGO.
MANY HAVE TRIED TO STOP MY FATHER, MR. WAYNE. THE MOUNTAINS ARE STREWN WITH THEIR BONES.
YES... BUT THIS MOST WORTHY ADVERSARY BROUGHT HIMSELF TO OUR VERY DOORSTEP, DAUGHTER. NONE BEFORE HAVE COME SO CLOSE.
SEE THE FIRE IN HIS EYES, FATHER! EVEN NOW, CAPTURED, HELPLESS, HE DOES NOT GIVE UP!
OF COURSE NOT. HE AND I ARE MUCH ALIKE, TALIA. WHEN HE WAS YOUNGER, I CONSIDERED HIM A WORTHY HEIR.
HEIR? ARE YOU AS MAD AS SOME SAY, RA'S? I'VE SPENT MY WHOLE LIFE FIGHTING YOUR KIND.

AND MANY TIMES FIGHTING *ME*, ADVERSARY, THOUGH YOU DID NOT *KNOW* IT.

MY *POWER* REACHES BACK OVER *MANY YEARS*, TO TOUCH THE LIFE OF THE *BATMAN* AT MANY PLACES!

YOU KNEW I WAS BATMAN--YET YOU THOUGHT I MIGHT BE A SUITABLE *REPLACEMENT* FOR "THE HEAD OF THE DEMON"?

MY... *WORK* REQUIRES A PARTICULAR TEMPERAMENT, ADVERSARY. A *ONENESS OF MIND* YOU AND I *SHARE*.

IF WE DO, IT'S THE *ONLY* THING WE SHARE, RA'S. YOU ARE *ANATHEMA* TO ME.

YOU THINK THIS ONLY BECAUSE YOUR MIND IS *NARROW*, MR. WAYNE.

YOU FAIL TO SEE WHAT A POWERFUL FORCE FOR *ORDER* MY FATHER IS IN THIS *CHAOTIC WORLD*.

ORDER? YES--I SUPPOSE YOU COULD CALL IT THAT. THE *ORDER OF DEATH*, THE *ORDER OF SLAVERY*.

YOU WILL FIND, I THINK, THAT I HAVE ENSLAVED NO ONE WHO DID NOT *WISH* IT, ADVERSARY.

YOU WOULD BE SURPRISED, PERHAPS, TO LEARN HOW MANY WILL SACRIFICE *FREEDOM* FOR *COMFORT*.

BUT NOW... I HAVE A *PROPOSITION* FOR YOU.

BEHOLD--THE *LAZARUS PIT*...

"NO, CLARK, THERE'S BEEN NO WORD.

IT'S BEEN ALMOST THREE WEEKS SINCE DAD WAS LAST SEEN, WALKING ALONE UP THAT HIMALAYAN PASS. IF HE WERE ANY OTHER MAN, I'D BE STARTING TO WORRY ABOUT HIM!
YES--YES, OF COURSE, I'LL LET YOU KNOW. AND NONE OF US WILL BE SURPRISED, I'M SURE, IF HE TURNS UP TOMORROW JUST IN TIME FOR THE WEDDING!
YES, I'LL SEE YOU THERE!
I'M PUTTING ON MY BEST, BRAVE FRONT, BUT A MAN DAD'S AGE, ALONE IN THOSE MOUNTAINS, ON SOME SECRET "MISSION"...
PENNY FOR YOUR THOUGHTS?
MOM! YOU CAME!
JUST BECAUSE YOUR FATHER AND I HAVE NOT SPOKEN IN YEARS DOESN'T MEAN I'M GOING TO MISS THE WEDDING OF MY ONLY SON!
IT'S WONDERFUL TO SEE YOU. KARA WILL BE DELIGHTED!
AH, YES! I HAVE A LITTLE SOMETHING FOR HER.
WAIT HERE... LET ME GET IT FROM MY LUGGAGE. YOU CAN TELL ME IF YOU THINK SHE'LL LIKE IT.
WELL, THERE'S A SURPRISE!
IT'S BEEN ALMOST FIVE YEARS SINCE MOM AND I LAST SAW EACH OTHER. I WAS BEGINNING TO THINK SHE'D TRANSFERRED HER ANGER AT DAD AND DICK TO ME...
I... HMM ...?

KARA! I THOUGHT YOU WANTED TO MAINTAIN TRADITION AND NOT LET ME SEE YOU BEFORE THE WEDDING!
YES--THAT DID SEEM LIKE A GOOD IDEA, FOR A WHILE.
BUT NOW I HAVE A BETTER IDEA.
HERE IT IS. I PICKED IT UP IN THAILAND A FEW MONTHS AGO.
B.J.?
??
OH, MY ..!!
"YOU REALLY MUST DO THIS?"

YES, MEI-LAI. THIS MOMENT HAS BEEN COMING FOR TWENTY YEARS.
TO AVOID IT NOW WOULD BE TO ATTEMPT TO SIDESTEP DESTINY.
BUT...HAVE YOU NOT SAID DESTINY IS WHAT WE MAKE IT, MY HUSBAND?
CAN YOU NOT FIND SOME OTHER WAY TO QUENCH THE FIRES THAT RAGE IN YOUR HEART?
NO.
I HAVE LEARNED MUCH IN THE YEARS SINCE YOU SAVED MY LIFE, MEI-LAI. I HAVE LEARNED TO BE TRANQUIL AS THE FOREST, BUT TO STOKE THE FLAMES WITHIN.
FOR SUCH PEACE AS I HAVE KNOWN IN THE LAST TEN YEARS, I HAVE ONLY YOU TO THANK.
WHATEVER HAPPENS--BE SURE OUR SON KNOWS HOW MUCH HIS FATHER LOVES HIM.
DON'T LET HIM GROW UP KNOWING THE PAIN I HAVE BORNE ALL MY LIFE!
"DEARLY BELOVED, WE ARE GATHERED HERE TODAY...

NO... "WE ARE GATHERED HERE TODAY..." ER... "...GATHERED HERE TODAY..."
PROBLEM, PADRE?
OH, MR. WAYNE! NO, NO PROBLEM. JUST--A TRIFLE NERVOUS, I'M AFRAID. I'VE PERFORMED THIS SERVICE HUNDREDS OF TIMES, BUT NEVER BEFORE SUCH AN AUGUST ASSEMBLAGE!
THE GOTHAM CITY A-LIST IS REPRESENTED HERE IN FULL, IT SEEMS!
DON'T LET 'EM RUFFLE YOU, FATHER! F. SCOTT FITZGERALD NOTWITHSTANDING, THE VERY RICH ARE NOT ALL THAT DIFFERENT FROM YOU AND ME!
ER--PERHAPS. BUT I DON'T SUPPOSE I REALLY NEED TO REMIND YOU, YOU ARE VERY RICH!
I'LL BE RICH IN THE ONLY WAY THAT MATTERS FATHER, ONCE KARA KENT IS MY WIFE.
HEADS UP, B.J.!
"HERE COMES THE BRIDE!"
WOW!
"THAT WAS BEAUTIFUL!

THE MOST BEAUTIFUL WEDDING I'VE EVER SEEN!
YOU MIGHT BE A BIT BIASED, MOM!
OH, I DON'T THINK SO, HONEY! AFTER ALL OUR YEARS AS REPORTERS, YOUR MOM AND I HAVE LEARNED TO BE OBJECTIVE!
I MUST AGREE! AND I MUST ALSO THANK YOU FOR INVITING ME, MY FRIENDS.
A SMALL REPAYMENT, DOCTOR. I SERIOUSLY DOUBT I'D BE HERE IF YOU HADN'T MADE IT POSSIBLE.
YES--OUR FAMILIES CAN NEVER PROPERLY SHOW OUR GRATITUDE.
OH--I WOULD NOT SAY THAT, MR. KENT.
IN FACT, I'D SAY I'M ABOUT TO RECEIVE PAYMENT IN FULL...
WHAT IN..??
CLARK!!

BLAST...OF...INTENSE... KRYPTONITE...RADIATION...
...CAN ...BARELY... BREATHE...
DON'T WORRY, SUPERMAN. I WANT YOU INCAPACITATED--BUT I DON'T WANT YOU DEAD.
NOT YET!
THAT SUIT BLOCKS MY X-RAY VISION, BUT THE TECHNOLOGY HAS LUTHOR WRITTEN ALL OVER IT!
ALL RIGHT, OLD MAN, IF YOU'VE COME FOR A FINAL SHOWDOWN...
...YOU'LL GET IT. AND REMEMBER, KRYPTONITE HURTS ME, BUT IT WILL TAKE A LONG TIME FOR IT TO STOP ME!
OH, I KNOW...
WHICH IS WHY I HAVE SOMETHING ELSE FOR YOU!!!
UNGH!!

NOW, ON WITH BUSINESS!
CLARK IS SUPERMAN ??
AFTER ALL THESE YEARS?!
DID YOU SEE?? KARA IS SUPERGIRL!
CLARK! CLARK ARE YOU...UNGH!
THUNG!
A FORCE-FIELD!

CLARK! LOIS!
GO! HELP KARA STOP LUTHOR!

YES... GOT TO GET AFTER THEM!
GOT TO FINISH LUTHOR ONCE AND FOR ALL!
A... DIFFICULT PROPOSITION, AT BEST, I WOULD SAY.

DR. HOLURT... YOU'RE INSIDE THE FORCE FIELD, TOO?
YES, MY DEAR. CLOSE BY, AS I HAVE ALWAYS BEEN.
LUTHOR!! THEN, WHO..??
THAT YOU WILL LEARN SOON ENOUGH, SUPER-MAN. TODAY WILL BE FULL OF PAINFUL LESSONS!
YOU WON'T GET AWAY WITH THIS, LUTHOR.
I HAVE BEEN "GETTING AWAY WITH IT" FOR LONGER THAN YOU COULD BEGIN TO IMAGINE, LOIS...
...IF ONLY BY ALLOWING YOUR HUSBAND TO CONTINUE HIS LITTLE MASQUERADE, WHEN I HAVE KNOWN FOR DECADES HE WAS SUPERMAN.
BUT THE TIME FOR SUCH THINGS IS BE-HIND US.
LUTHOR! NO! YOUR FIGHT IS WITH ME! DON'T HURT HER!
OH, I THINK I CAN PROMISE YOU THIS WILL NOT HURT AT ALL, SUPERMAN.
SNAP
LOOK! LUTHOR IS... BEAMING AWAY!
ANIMAL! MONSTER!
I'LL KILL YOU FOR THIS! OR I'LL DIE TRYING!
SAVE YOUR BREATH, SUPERMAN. TODAY IS NOT YOUR DAY TO DIE.
I WANT YOU ALIVE, TO SEE YOUR WHOLE FAMILY PERISH! AND NOW THAT YOUR WIFE IS DEAD...

"...IT IS TIME FOR YOUR DAUGHTER TO JOIN HER!"
THERE SHE IS! AS I EXPECTED, THE IMPACT HAS NOT DIMINISHED HER ARROGANCE!
WHY DON'T YOU JUST SURRENDER, LUTHOR? YOU KNOW YOUR TECHNOLOGY CAN NEVER BE A MATCH FOR MY POWERS.
I'LL MOLD THAT SUIT INTO THE BARS OF YOUR CELL!
YOU MIGHT JUST DO THAT, KARA...
...IF THE POWER WAS IN THE SUIT!
JOEL!!

YES--JOEL! YOUR DEAR, DEAD BROTHER! DISAPPOINTED TO SEE ME ALIVE AND WELL, KARA?
NO! BUT... HOW? WHY ??

"MY OWN MEN TRIED TO KILL ME, KARA. THEY SHOT ME IN THE BACK, TOOK MY DOGTAGS, LEFT ME FOR DEAD.

"BUT I WAS FOUND, LYING THERE IN THE BLOODY MUD.
"FOUND BY A BEAUTIFUL ANGEL WHO SAW BEYOND THE WAR THAT MADE ENEMIES OF OUR COUNTRIES.

"SHE NURSED ME BACK TO HEALTH. SHE GAVE ME BACK MY LIFE.
"AND WHEN I WAS AT LAST ABLE TO GET IN TOUCH WITH THE ONLY MAN WHO HAD BEEN A TRUE FATHER TO ME...

...SHE CAME BACK HOME WITH US. BACK TO BECOME MY WIFE.
YES--YOU HAVE A SISTER-IN-LAW, KARA. A LITTLE SOMETHING TO WARM YOUR HEART, BEFORE I TEAR IT OUT OF YOU!
LUTHOR..? YOU... YOU THINK OF LUTHOR AS SOME-HOW... YOUR FATHER..??
BUT HE'S A MURDERER! A MONSTER!!
NO! HE'S A GREAT MAN! AND THE ONLY MAN WHO HAS EVER BEEN HONEST WITH ME!

BUT YOU CAN'T SEE THAT, CAN YOU, KARA? YOU WERE THE DAUGHTER. YOU WERE ALLOWED TO KEEP THE POWERS THAT ARE OUR KRYPTONIAN HERITAGE.
OUR FATHER DIDN'T EXPOSE YOU TO GOLD KRYPTONITE SO YOU WOULD BE BORN A HELPLESS MORTAL!
WHAT?!?
BUT IT WAS LUTHOR WHO EXPOSED MOM TO THE GOLD K WHILE SHE WAS PREGNANT WITH YOU!
LIES! THE LIES I BELIEVED FOR THE FIRST TEN YEARS OF MY LIFE!
UNTIL LUTHOR FOUND ME, AND TOLD ME THE TRUTH! TOLD ME SUPERMAN WAS JEALOUS! THAT HE WAS AFRAID I'D BE GREATER THAN HIM!
BUT HE KNEW A GIRL WOULD NEVER BE HIS EQUAL. HE KNEW YOU'D BE THE SNIVELING LITTLE LAPDOG YOU ARE!
WHAT HE NEVER COUNTED ON WAS LUTHOR FINDING A WAY TO GIVE ME THE POWERS I DESERVED!

THE POWER TO KILL YOU!!
"THERE! IN THE CENTER OF THAT MASS OF DESTRUCTION!

KARA!!!
KARA...??
...KARA...
"IT WENT PRECISELY ACCORDING TO PLAN, SIR.

I MUST CONFESS, THOUGH... AT THE LAST MOMENT, I FELT ALMOST A... HESITATION.
AS IF I DIDN'T REALLY WANT TO KILL HER.
I'M SURE YOU DIDN'T. YOU STILL HAVE YOUR FATHER'S HEART, JOEL. EVEN AFTER ALL THESE YEARS.
NO! IT COULDN'T HAVE BEEN THAT! I WANT NO PART OF HIM! NO PART OF HIS LIES!
BUT... UHH... I FEEL... STRANGE. LEX... WHAT..?
NOTHING UNEXPECTED. THE FORMULA I CONCOCTED TO GIVE YOU POWERS LIKE YOUR FATHER'S--I ANTICIPATED IT WOULD HAVE THIS EFFECT WITHIN FIVE HOURS.
EFFECT... WHAT... EFFECT..?
REMEMBER WHEN YOU CONFRONTED YOUR FATHER WITH YOUR KNOWLEDGE THAT HE WAS SUPERMAN? REMEMBER HOW HE TOLD YOU HE WISHED HE COULD GIVE YOU THE POWERS THE GOLD K HAD TAKEN AWAY, BUT THAT HE COULD NOT?
THAT THERE WAS NO FORMULA KNOWN WHICH COULD GIVE A HUMAN SUCH POWERS WITHOUT KILLING THEM?
A... LIE. THE... FIRST OF... SO MANY... HE TOLD... ME...
WELL, NO, NOT PRECISELY.

YOU SEE, MY POOR, FOOLISH, GULLIBLE BOY...
YOUR FATHER HAS NEVER LIED TO YOU. WHILE I, ON THE OTHER HAND, HAVE ALWAYS LIED...
JOEL...?
J-JOEL...? ALIVE...?
NOT ANYMORE. I SAID YOU WOULD SEE YOUR WHOLE FAMILY DIE TODAY, DID I NOT?
MONSTER! I'LL...
OH, FIDDLE-FADDLE, SUPERMAN!
YOU CAN'T IMAGINE I WOULD REALLY BE HERE, IN PERSON? I AM MILES AWAY, IN A PLACE YOU WILL NOT FIND SO EASILY AS YOU DID THIS.
AFTER ALL, I WANTED YOU TO FIND THIS PLACE!
S-SUPERMAN..?

WHO...?
I AM MEI-LAI KENT, SUPERMAN. YOUR SON WAS MY HUSBAND--AND THIS IS YOUR GRANDSON.
GRANDSON..? Y-YES, I CAN SEE WITH MY MICROSCOPIC VISION. THE GENETIC MATCH IS EXACT.
BUT... LIKE JOEL ... HE HAS NO SUPER POWERS.
OH, LORD! I HEARD EVERYTHING LUTHOR AND JOEL SAID... HEARD IT WITH MY SUPER-HEARING AS I APPROACHED THIS LAIR.
LUTHOR WAS ABLE TO TURN JOEL AGAINST ME--BECAUSE OF WHAT I FEARED WHEN I LEARNED JOEL WOULD HAVE NO POWERS.
BECAUSE OF THE TERRIBLE BURDEN OF GROWING UP THE POWERLESS SON OF SUPERMAN.
NOW... THIS BABY... MY GRANDSON...
...WILL NEVER HAVE TO CARRY THAT BURDEN, CLARK.
WE BOTH LOST EVERYTHING TODAY. EVERYTHING THAT MATTERS.
YET, IN THIS CHILD, PERHAPS WE'VE BOTH BEEN GIVEN SOMETHING. A SECOND CHANCE.
IN THIS CHILD, PERHAPS, WE CAN BUILD THE TRUE UNION OF OUR FAMILIES...
...AND A HOPE FOR A BETTER TOMORROW!

1989
Crime and Punishment

WE HAVE NO *CHOICE*, MR. PRESIDENT.

LUTHOR RIGGED IT SO THAT IMAGE WAS TRANSMITTED WORLDWIDE, AT THE MOMENT IT HAPPENED.
EVERYONE WHO WAS IN FRONT OF A TV SET, AND EVERYONE WHO HAS SEEN THE COUNTLESS REBROADCASTS, KNOWS SUPERMAN IS A MURDERER.
I CAN'T BELIEVE IT!
THERE'S NO DOUBT, MR. PRESIDENT. THE BODY HAS BEEN LOCATED AND IDENTIFIED.
THERE IS NO QUESTION THAT IT IS--WAS REALLY LEX LUTHOR.
I DON'T KNOW WHICH IS HARDER TO BELIEVE--THAT THAT MENACE HAS FINALLY BEEN ENDED...
...OR THAT HE WAS ABLE TO DRIVE SUPERMAN TO SUCH DEPTHS OF MADNESS AND DESPAIR...
WE ALL KNOW IT'S BEEN DOWNHILL FOR SUPERMAN SINCE HIS FAMILY WAS MURDERED BY LUTHOR, MR. PRESIDENT.
YES -- THE POP PSYCHOLOGISTS HAVE BEEN PRODUCING VOLUMES ON SUPERMAN'S MENTAL STATE EVER SINCE.
I READ SOME OF THEM. THE LOSS OF HIS FAMILY, THE EXPOSURE OF HIS SECRET IDENTITY...
ENOUGH TO DRIVE EVEN THE BEST OF US MAD, I SUPPOSE.
VERY WELL--I AM COMPELLED TO AGREE WITH YOU. THERE IS ONLY ONE THING WE CAN DO, NOW.

TE-ENN HUT!
MR. PRESIDENT-- YOU UNDERSTAND THE PROTOCOLS...
YES, CORPORAL. I HAVE TO PROVE I'M REALLY WHO I APPEAR TO BE, BEFORE I CAN GET INTO THAT ELEVATOR.
VOICE IDENTIFICATION CODE ZERO ZERO ALPHA.
PRESIDENT HAROLD JORDAN REQUIRING ACCESS TO ZONE OMEGA.
VOICE, PALM AND RETINAL SCANS CONFIRMED.
WELCOME, MR. PRESIDENT.
JUST HOW FAR DOWN DOES THIS ELEVATOR GO, MR. PRESIDENT?
I CAN FEEL THE PRESSURE CHANGING!
ALMOST A MILE, GERRY.
AND THAT'S JUST THE BEGINNING.
NEXT, WE DRIVE FOR ABOUT TEN MILES.
WELCOME MR. PRESIDENT, GENTLEMEN, LADY.

WHAT DO YOU SUPPOSE THE TAXPAYERS WOULD SAY IF THEY KNEW ABOUT THIS PLACE?
IF THEY KNEW WHAT IT COST THEM?
NOT MUCH, I EXPECT.
NOT NOW.
THIS INSTALLATION WAS CREATED IN ANSWER TO PERHAPS THE GREATEST SECURITY PROBLEM WE HAVE EVER FACED--
--HOW DO YOU KEEP SUPERMAN OUT OF A PLACE HE DOESN'T WANT TO BE KEPT OUT OF?
LUCKY IT NEVER CAME TO THAT!
NO... THAT WOULD HAVE BEEN VERY MUCH WHAT WE USED TO CALL A "TEST TO DESTRUCTION," BACK IN MY TEST PILOT DAYS.
STAND BACK NOW, WHILE I DEACTIVATE THE LASERS.
EVERYTHING IN HERE IS BASED ON OUR MOST DETAILED STUDIES OF SUPERMAN'S PHYSIOLOGY..
AND THE LAST PART, OF COURSE, TAPS THE VERY THING THIS WAS ALL BUILT TO PROTECT.

THERE'S ENOUGH KRYPTONITE RADIATION BEING GENERATED IN THIS PIT TO KILL EVEN A HUMAN BEING WHO IS EXPOSED FOR MORE THAN A FEW SECONDS.
IT TOOK YEARS TO DEVELOP THESE RADIATION SUITS--AND KEY THEM TO SELF-DESTRUCT SHOULD SUPERMAN TRY TO WEAR ONE.
AND NOW, THE LAST STEP.
CALLING UP THE CONTAINMENT UNIT FROM INSIDE A CUBE OF TRI-TITANIUM ALLOY MORE THAN A MILE ON A SIDE!
NONE OF US EVER THOUGHT IT WOULD COME TO THIS, OF COURSE!
SUPERMAN GAVE ONE OF MY PREDECESSORS THIS FRAGMENT OF KRYPTONITE "TO USE ON HIM IF HE SHOULD EVER GO MAD.
HE SAID AT THE TIME, "IF YOU CAN'T TRUST THE PRESIDENT OF THE UNITED STATES, WHO CAN YOU TRUST?"
WASN'T IT NIXON HE GAVE THE GREEN K TO..?
YES. ANOTHER SMALL IRONY. NOW...
OH MY LORD ..!!!

"IT'S GONE !!!!"
I REALLY HATED BREAKING INTO THE WHITE HOUSE LIKE THAT...
...BUT SOMEHOW I KNEW HAL JORDAN WOULD NEVER WILLINGLY SURRENDER THE KRYPTONITE TO ME.
NOT WITH MY PRESENT REPUTATION.
THERE'S THE GIANT KEY SUPERMAN DISGUISED TO LOOK LIKE AN AIRCRAFT DIRECTION INDICATOR.
NO WAY I COULD EVER MOVE IT.
BUT I WON'T NEED TO.
SUPERMAN TRUSTED MY FAMILY ENOUGH TO TELL THREE GENERATIONS OF BATMEN THE SECRET WAYS TO ENTER HIS FORTRESS OF SOLITUDE.

IN FACT, WHEN THE PATH IS KNOWN...
...PASSAGE IS NOT A WHOLE LOT HARDER THAN STROLLING THROUGH GOTHAM PARK.
OR THROUGH A KEYHOLE!
ALTHOUGH... I MIGHT HAVE EXPECTED SUPERMAN TO HAVE MODIFIED THE FORTRESS'S DEFENSES, GIVEN THE PRESENT CIRCUMSTANCES.
IS HE NOT EXPECTING ME...?

IS HE NOT EVEN HERE? MY TRI-DI SCANNER CANNOT DETECT HIS UNIQUE PHYSIOLOGICAL SIGNATURE ANYWHERE IN THE FORTRESS.
BUT IT ONLY MAKES SENSE THAT HE WOULD GO TO GROUND HERE. HE CREATED THIS PLACE TO BE IMPENETRABLE.
LOOKS LIKE I'M GOING TO HAVE TO DRAW HIM OUT OF HIDING.
AND THE BEST WAY TO DO THAT...
...IS TO GO RIGHT TO THE HEART OF THE MATTER.
BOOM

SUPERMAN ALWAYS WAS TOO MUCH OF A SENTIMENTALIST. THIS STRUCTURE IS MORE LIKE A GIANT CLUBHOUSE THAN THE BATCAVE EVER WAS!
IN ITS OWN WAY, THE FORTRESS IS AS BIG A WEAKNESS AS THE KRYPTONITE IN MY UTILITY BELT!
HE WON'T BE ABLE TO STAY IN HIDING WHILE I SYSTEMATICALLY TRASH ALL HIS MEMENTOS.
LET'S SEE WHAT'S THROUGH THIS DOOR...
OH NO...

...KARA...
BATMAN.
STOP!

PULLING YOUR PUNCHES, CLARK?
A MISTAKE. YOU SHOULD HAVE TAKEN ME DOWN WITH THE FIRST HIT.
NOT AN OPTION, BRUCE.
JUST AS YOUR CONTINUED ASSAULT ON MY HOME IS NOT AN OPTION.
NOTHING I ENJOYED, I ASSURE YOU.
JUST AS I CAN TELL YOU'RE NOT ENJOYING THIS FIGHT. OR ARE YOU JUST TOYING WITH ME?

NO, BRUCE.
I'M GIVING IT MY ALL. BUT MY ALL ISN'T WHAT IT USED TO BE!
GREAT SCOTT !!
YOUR FACE! WHAT..?!?
YES -- PAIN. BLOOD. AND I WOULD IMAGINE NO SMALL AMOUNT OF BRUISING.
SOMETHING I'LL HAVE TO GET USED TO NOW, I SUPPOSE. NOW THAT I AM NO LONGER SUPERHUMAN!
CARE TO... EXPLAIN THAT, CLARK?
"FOR WHAT IT'S WORTH...
"IT BEGAN FIVE DAYS AGO, WHEN A DECADE OF SEARCHING FINALLY BORE FRUIT..."
HE'S THERE. IN THAT TOWER. HE DOESN'T EVEN SEEM TO BE TRYING TO HIDE FROM ME!
LUTHOR!!
WELCOME, SUPERMAN.
IT HAS BEEN SUCH A LONG TIME!

YOU WON'T THINK IT NEARLY LONG ENOUGH, WHEN I'M DONE WITH YOU, LUTHOR!
YOU'RE GOING TO PAY FOR YOUR CRIMES AGAINST HUMANITY--AGAINST MY FAMILY.
SPARE ME THE MORAL OUTRAGE, SUPERMAN.
YOU HAVE BEEN FAR TOO DERELICT IN YOUR SELF-APPOINTED DUTIES TO PLAY THAT TUNE!
LOOK WHAT'S HAPPENED WHILE YOU WASTED TIME SEARCHING FOR ME!
YOUR "PAL" JIMMY OLSEN, KILLED IN A MYSTERIOUS BLAST.
"HIS WIDOW, LUCY, GUNNED DOWN BY BANK ROBBERS.
"THEIR SON, CLARK, AND HIS WIFE AND CHILDREN DRIVEN OFF A CLIFF ROAD BY A RUNAWAY TRUCK.
"MAYOR PEREGRINE WHITE JR. SLAIN BY ASSASSINS!
"AND A DOZEN OTHERS, OF COURSE. ALL CLOSE TO YOU. ALL DEAD."

TH-THOSE WERE NOT COMPUTER RE-CREATIONS! THAT WAS ACTUAL FOOTAGE OF MY FRIENDS DYING!
HOW..?
YOU FIEND! WASN'T SLAUGHTERING MY FAMILY ENOUGH FOR AH-GH!
PROBLEM, SUPERMAN?
...COULD I POSSIBLY HAVE SUCH IMAGES, UNLESS I WAS SOMEHOW PRECOGNITIVE?
OR--UNLESS I WAS THE ONE WHO ENGINEERED EACH OF THOSE UNTIMELY DEATHS!
MY ARM! PULLING YOU OUT OF THAT CHAIR ALMOST DISLOCATED MY SHOULDER!
WELL, YES, I EXPECT IT WOULD!
I AM DECIDEDLY SHRUNKEN FROM MY GREATEST BULK, SUPERMAN, BUT STILL, TRYING TO LIFT MY WEIGHT WITH ONE HAND WOULD STRAIN ANY MERE MORTAL.
WHICH IS, OF COURSE, WHAT YOU ARE NOW, SUPERMAN.
OR DIDN'T YOU NOTICE THE RARE STONE I HAVE MOUNTED IN MY CUFFLINKS...?
GOLD KRYPTON-ITE!

YES--AS YOU CAN SEE, THIS FINAL PLOT HAS A GREAT MANY LAYERS TO IT, SUPERMAN!
BUT... YOU CAN WALK ...?

OH, YES. I AM OLD AND WEAK, SUPERMAN--BUT NOT YET THAT INFIRM. THE CHAIR IS MERELY TO CONSERVE ENERGY.
SOMETHING I WILL NEVER NEED DO AGAIN, ONCE I HAVE TRANSFERRED MY MIND INTO YOUR BODY!
WHAT...? WHAT ARE YOU TALKING ABOUT, LUTHOR??

OH-- AND THAT...
THIS GUISE HAS SERVED ME WELL ENOUGH FOR THE PAST FIFTY YEARS, BUT NOW THE MOMENT HAS COME FOR YOUR UTTER DEFEAT, I WANT YOU TO KNOW WHO IT REALLY WAS WHO BESTED YOU.
LOOK INTO MY EYES, SUPERMAN. LOOK DEEP INTO MY EYES...
NO! IT CAN'T BE!
THE ULTRA-HUMANITE!

"YES... HALF A CENTURY AGO, AFTER I WAS BRIEFLY BESTED BY YOURSELF AND THE BAT-MAN AT THE METROPOLIS WORLD'S FAIR...
"...MY ROBOTS FOUND ME, BROKEN AND DYING IN THE WRECKAGE OF MY ESCAPE SHIP.

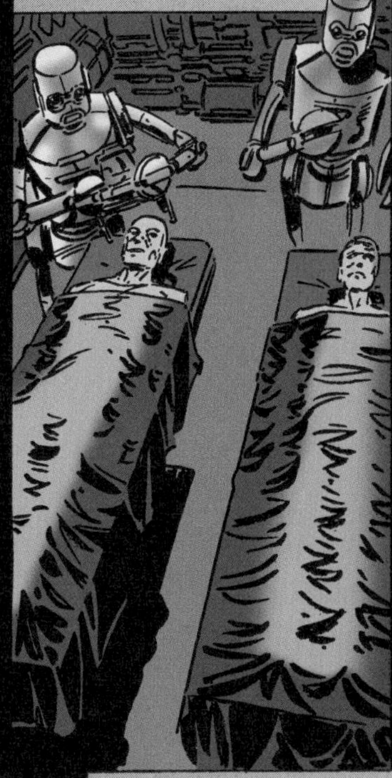
"BY CHANCE, THE HENCHMAN I CALLED ELL HAD SUFFERED INJURIES ALMOST PRECISELY THE OPPOSITE OF MY OWN.
"WHILE MY BODY WAS BROKEN, IT WAS HIS BRAIN WHICH HAD BEEN DESTROYED.

"USING TECHNIQUES I HAD EARLIER PERFECTED, MY ROBOTS TRANSPLANTED MY BRAIN INTO ELL'S BODY.
"BUT THERE WAS AN ACCIDENT. THE TRANSFER WAS IMPERFECT, AND MY BRAIN WAS TRAPPED IN THAT FORM!
AND... AS I GUESSED AT THE TIME, "ELL" WAS REALLY... LEX LUTHOR, MY OLD NEMESIS FROM MY DAYS AS SUPERBOY!
YES. HAVING YOU BELIEVE ME TO BE LUTHOR ALL THESE YEARS GAVE ME A SLIGHT ADVANTAGE, SUPERMAN.
AS DID KNOWING, BUT NOT REVEALING YOUR SECRET IDENTITY.
NOW... WITH ONE STROKE I CAN ELIMINATE MY GREATEST ENEMY, AND AT THE SAME TIME GAIN ALL HIS POWER!
THIS DEVICE WILL ACCOMPLISH WHAT EVEN THE MOST DELICATE SURGERY COULD NOT--EXCHANGING MY MIND FOR YOURS!
I DON'T THINK SO, ULTRA!
GAH!
OH--I'M SORRY, SUPERMAN--DID I NEGLECT TO MENTION THAT YOU ARE NOW SURROUNDED BY BARS OF INVISIBLE ENERGY?
THEY WILL HOLD YOU CAPTIVE UNTIL I CAN COMPLETE THE TRANSFER.
HE'S GOT ME! HE'S REALLY, REALLY GOT ME, THIS TIME!
WITHOUT MY POWERS THERE'S NO WAY TO BREACH THIS FORCEFIELD CAGE, NO WAY TO REACH ULTRA...
UNLESS...

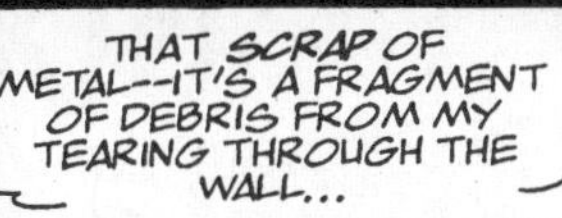
THAT SCRAP OF METAL--IT'S A FRAGMENT OF DEBRIS FROM MY TEARING THROUGH THE WALL...
...AND EVEN WITHOUT SUPER POWERS, I CAN PUT IT TO GOOD USE, IF I CAN DELAY THE HUMANITE A FEW SECONDS LONGER.

THERE'S ONE LAST THING YOU CAN TELL ME, ULTRA, BEFORE YOU HAVE YOUR VENGEANCE.
I SEARCHED THIS WHOLE PLANET FOR YOU. HOW WERE YOU ABLE TO ELUDE ME FOR TEN YEARS?
BY SKIPPING OVER THAT DECADE, SUPER-MAN.
I DISCOVERED A UNIQUE FIELD EFFECT GENERATED WHEN ACETYLSALICYLIC ACID IS IRRADIATED AT A 108 MEGA-HERTZ FREQUENCY.

I CREATED A TIME PORTAL, AND SIMPLY STEPPED INTO THE FUTURE.
BY MY OWN CLOCK, I ARRIVED HERE ONLY TWO DAYS AGO. A QUICK CHECK REVEALED THAT ALL MY MACHINATIONS HAD PLAYED THEMSELVES OUT AS PLANNED...

...AND IT WAS THEN ONLY A MATTER OF WAITING FOR YOU TO FIND ME.
NOW, I NEED BUT TO DON THIS ENCEPHALO-TRANSFER HELMET...
...AND IN A MATTER OF SECONDS ALL YOUR POWER WILL BE MINE!

OR NOT...
EVEN WITHOUT SUPER STRENGTH I CAN FLIP THIS SHARD INTO MY HAND...

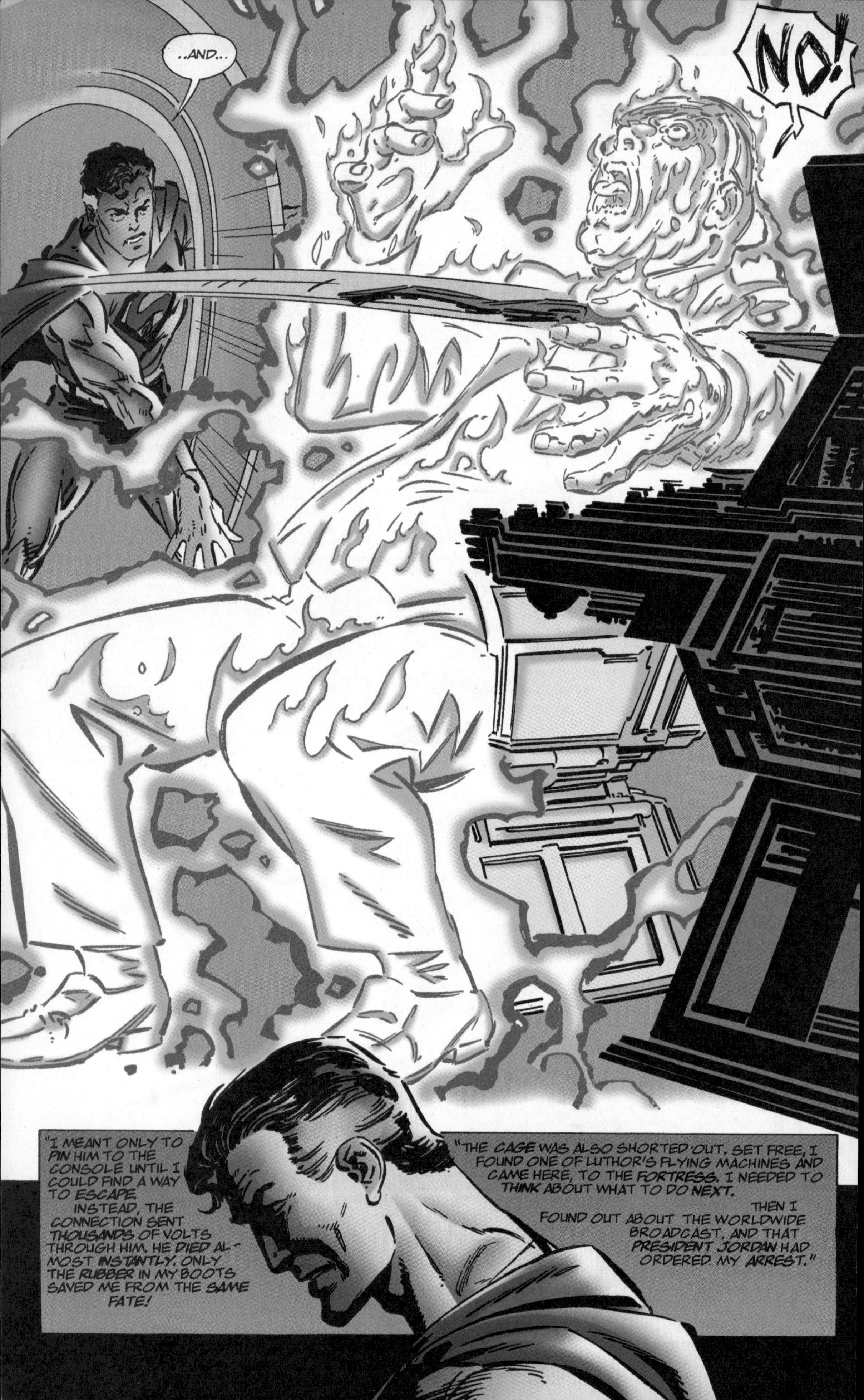

..AND...
NO!
"I MEANT ONLY TO PIN HIM TO THE CONSOLE UNTIL I COULD FIND A WAY TO ESCAPE.
INSTEAD, THE CONNECTION SENT THOUSANDS OF VOLTS THROUGH HIM. HE DIED ALMOST INSTANTLY. ONLY THE RUBBER IN MY BOOTS SAVED ME FROM THE SAME FATE!
"THE CAGE WAS ALSO SHORTED OUT. SET FREE, I FOUND ONE OF LUTHOR'S FLYING MACHINES AND CAME HERE, TO THE FORTRESS. I NEEDED TO THINK ABOUT WHAT TO DO NEXT.
THEN I FOUND OUT ABOUT THE WORLDWIDE BROADCAST, AND THAT PRESIDENT JORDAN HAD ORDERED MY ARREST."

BUT--HOW WAS LUTHOR ABLE TO TRANSMIT THAT IMAGE ACROSS THE GLOBE IF HE WAS *DEAD?*
SOME KIND OF *CONTINGENCY PLAN*, BRUCE. EVEN WITH HIS COLOSSAL *EGO*, THE ULTRA-HUMANITE STILL PLANNED A WAY TO DEFEAT ME, EVEN IF I BEAT HIM.
ULTRA ASSUMED THE ONLY WAY HE COULD *DIE* WAS BY MY HAND--AND HIS COMPUTERS WERE PROGRAMMED TO *TAPE* THE WHOLE ENCOUNTER, THEN *DESTROY* ALL BUT THE MOMENT OF HIS *DEATH.*

IT WAS ALL A *SETUP!* EVERY MOMENT *CHOREOGRAPHED* BY ULTRA.
BUT IT WAS CLEARLY *SELF-DEFENSE*, CLARK.
AND HOW DO I *PROVE* THAT, BRUCE? THE *TAPE* IS GONE, THE *CIRCUITRY* OF ULTRA'S MIND-TRANSFERENCE DEVICE *FUSED* BEYOND RECOGNITION.
AND EVEN WERE THAT *NOT* THE CASE--WHEN I APPEAR BEFORE THE *WORLD COURT* I INTEND TO PLEAD...

...*GUILTY*, YOUR HONORS.
"GUILTY"?

BUT, SUPERMAN, THE BATMAN HAS ALREADY TOLD THE COURT YOU ACTED IN *SELF-DEFENSE.*
DID I, YOUR HONOR?

YEARS AGO, I SWORE AN *OATH AGAINST KILLING*, AND FOR MOST OF MY LIFE I HAVE *HONORED* THAT OATH ABOVE ALL OTHERS.
BUT I *HATED* LUTHOR--HATED WHAT HE HAD DONE TO *ME*, TO MY *FAMILY*. I CANNOT BE SURE IT WAS NOT THAT *HATRED* WHICH GUIDED MY HAND AT THE LAST MOMENT.
IN MY OWN MIND, I CANNOT BE *ABSOLUTELY CERTAIN* IT WAS NOT *COLD BLOODED MURDER!*

VERY WELL, SUPERMAN... WE CONCUR. BUT IN LIGHT OF YOUR PREVIOUS SERVICE TO ALL MANKIND, WE SENTENCE YOU TO A PRISON TERM NOT TO EXCEED TEN YEARS.
HOWEVER, YOU PRESENT US WITH A UNIQUE PROBLEM, SUPERMAN. STRIPPED OF YOUR POWERS, YOU WOULD NOT SURVIVE A DAY IN THE GENERAL POPULACE OF ANY PRISON...
...YET TO CONDEMN YOU TO SOLITARY CONFINEMENT WOULD BE CRUEL AND UNUSUAL PUNISHMENT.
WE HAVE A SOLUTION TO THAT, YOUR HONORS.
THE LAW
THIS KRYPTONIAN ARTIFACT... THE PHANTOM ZONE PROJECTOR!
AS WITH CRIMINALS ON MY NATIVE KRYPTON, THIS DEVICE CAN BE USED TO SEND ME INTO A GHOST-LIKE STATE.
VERY WELL--WE ACCEPT THAT AS A FITTING PUNISHMENT.
BATMAN --WILL YOU...
...SERVE AS EXECUTIONER? YES, YOUR HONORS.
SUPERMAN...
DON'T SAY ANYTHING, OLD FRIEND. THIS IS FOR THE BEST.
I WILL SEE YOU AGAIN IN TEN YEARS.
PERHAPS BY THEN, YOU WILL HAVE MADE A BETTER WORLD!

1999
Beginnings and Endings
WELCOME, BATMAN.
I HAVE WAITED A LONG TIME FOR THIS MOMENT.

YOU WON'T THINK IT'S LONG ENOUGH BY HALF BY THE TIME I'M FINISHED WITH YOU, FRIEND.
MY FATHER DISAPPEARED TWENTY YEARS AGO, SEARCHING FOR YOU--BUT DON'T EXPECT ME TO CONVENIENTLY DO THE SAME!
I HAVE NO DESIRE TO SEE YOU DISAPPEAR, BATMAN.
QUITE THE OPPOSITE, IN FACT. I HOPE TO SEE YOU TAKE MY PLACE HERE!
TAKE YOUR ...?
I'D HEARD YOU WERE A MADMAN, BUT I HAD NO IDEA YOUR DEMENTIA WAS SO DEEP...!
THIS IS NOT MADNESS, BATMAN.
HEAR HIM OUT!
I'LL LISTEN--BUT I SHOULD WARN YOU, THERE'S NO WAY ON EARTH YOUR STORY WILL BE GOOD ENOUGH!
OH--I THINK IT WILL, BATMAN.
LET ME BEGIN BY TELLING YOU EXACTLY WHAT HAPPENED TO YOUR FATHER.

THIS IS THE FIRST TIME IN TWO DECADES THAT I HAVE ENTERED THIS ROOM, BATMAN.
THIS IS THE LAZARUS PIT. BY MEANS OF ITS MINGLING OF SCIENCE AND MYSTICISM IT IS POSSIBLE TO GAIN A KIND OF IMMORTALITY.
IT WAS HERE THAT TWO STORIES ENDED, AND A THIRD BEGAN!
I HAVE USED THE LAZARUS PIT TO EXTEND MY LIFETIME CENTURIES BEYOND THE NORM, ADVERSARY.
BUT THERE IS A GREAT TOLL WITH EACH USAGE. A PENALTY TO BE PAID IN MADNESS.
ARE YOU BLAMING THIS GOO FOR YOUR ACTIONS, RA'S?
NOT AT ALL.
BUT I HAVE SPENT MUCH OF MY LONG LIFE STUDYING THE LAZARUS PIT--SEEKING TO EXTRACT ITS GIFTS WITHOUT PAYING THE PRICE.
AND, AFTER MANY YEARS, I BELIEVE I HAVE FOUND THAT WAY.
A SINGLE MIND, A SINGLE SOUL IS NOT STRONG ENOUGH TO WITHSTAND THE RIGORS OF REGENERATION WITHOUT AT LEAST A TEMPORARY MADNESS.
HOWEVER, IF TWO ENTER THE PIT TOGETHER, THE FORCE OF THEIR LIVES WILL BE MELDED TOGETHER.
ONE WILL PERISH, BUT THE OTHER WILL BECOME IMMORTAL!
YOU'RE NOT SUGGESTING--THAT I WILLINGLY CLIMB INTO THAT STUFF WITH YOU?
THAT I SACRIFICE MY LIFE TO GIVE YOU IMMORTALITY?

IN FACT-- I AM NOT, ADVERSARY.
TWO ENTER THE PIT--AND ONLY ONE EMERGES. BUT I HAVE NO WAY OF GUARANTEEING WHICH ONE.
THIS IS MY CHALLENGE TO YOU, MR. WAYNE. YOU CAME HERE TO DESTROY THE "HEAD OF THE DEMON."
WILL YOU RISK YOUR LIFE AGAINST A CHANCE TO GAIN THAT END, AND LIVE FOREVER!?
RISK DEATH -- OR DIE LIKE A DOG AT THE HANDS OF YOUR MEN?
THAT'S HARDLY A CHOICE, IS IT, RA'S?
EXCELLENT! YOU ARE EVERY BIT AS WORTHY AS I HAD HOPED!
MY DAUGHTER, TALIA, WILL OPERATE THE CONTROLS THAT LOWER THIS PLATFORM INTO THE PIT.
SHE WILL ALSO SHOOT YOU, SHOULD YOU DECIDE AT THE LAST MOMENT TO CHANGE YOUR MIND!
AND YOU APPROVE OF THIS, TALIA? YOU ENDORSE YOUR FATHER'S MADNESS?
A LOYAL DAUGHTER CAN DO NO LESS, MR. WAYNE.

PREPARE YOURSELF, ADVERSARY. AS THE NAME SUGGESTS, IT IS NOT NORMALLY THE CUSTOM TO IMMERSE LIVING SUBJECTS IN THE LAZARUS PIT.
THERE MAY BE... INDESCRIBABLE AGONY.
PAIN AND I ARE NO STRANGERS, RA'S.
IT HAS BEEN MY CONSTANT COMPANION FOR MANY YEARS!

UH-HH!! DO... YOU FEEL... IT... ADVERSARY..?
THE TORMENT BEGINS...
I'VE FELT--UNGH!--WORSE THAN THIS IN A FISTFIGHT WITH THE JOKER!

NO! THE PAIN IS TOO GREAT!
IT IS AS I FEARED! NO MORTAL CAN BEAR THE PROCESS..!!
NOT...SO FAST... RA'S!
YOU DEALT THIS HAND...
...BUT I INTEND TO PLAY IT!

...FATHER..??

AI-EEE!!

FATHER !!!

WE HAD NO WAY OF KNOWING WHAT TO EXPECT...
FATHER COULD NOT INSTRUCT ME AS TO WHAT I MUST DO.

ON MY OWN INITIATIVE I MUST RAISE THE PLATFORM!

THERE IS ONLY ONE OF THEM..!
FATHER..?

NO.

IT... WASN'T RA'S AL GHUL WHO EMERGED FROM THE PIT?
NO, BATMAN.
IT WAS BRUCE WAYNE!
D-DAD...?!?
I THOUGHT YOU WERE DEAD! I WAS SURE YOU WERE DEAD!
TWENTY YEARS WITHOUT SO MUCH AS A WORD...!
NOT WITHOUT GOOD REASON, SON.
RA'S WAS GONE, I WAS IMMORTAL...

"...AND I REALIZED I HAD A BIG JOB AHEAD OF ME!
FROM THIS CONTROL CENTER I AM ABLE TO MONITOR OPERATIONS IN THE WORLDWIDE NETWORK RA'S AL GHUL CREATED.
A CRIMINAL NETWORK--OF WHICH YOU ARE NOW THE HEAD..??
YES -- WHEN I ASSUMED CONTROL, WITH TALIA AT MY SIDE, THIS WAS, INDEED, A VAST CRIMINAL ORGANIZATION.
A POWERFUL SECRET GOVERNMENT THAT CROSSED ALL BORDERS, THAT WORKED VIRTUALLY WITHOUT HINDRANCE IN EVERY COUNTRY ON EARTH!
DO YOU NOT SEE, SON, THE OPPORTUNITY THAT PRESENTED?
NO.
ENLIGHTEN ME, FATHER.

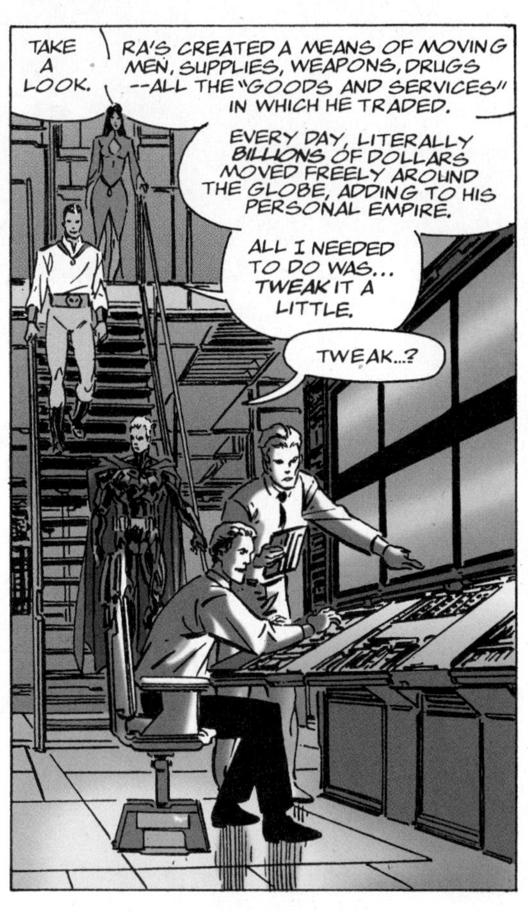
TAKE A LOOK.
RA'S CREATED A MEANS OF MOVING MEN, SUPPLIES, WEAPONS, DRUGS --ALL THE "GOODS AND SERVICES" IN WHICH HE TRADED.
EVERY DAY, LITERALLY BILLIONS OF DOLLARS MOVED FREELY AROUND THE GLOBE, ADDING TO HIS PERSONAL EMPIRE.
ALL I NEEDED TO DO WAS... TWEAK IT A LITTLE.
TWEAK...?

YES. YOU'VE BEEN SO DEDICATED TO TRACKING DOWN THE HEAD OF THE DEMON, YOU DIDN'T NOTICE HOW THE BODY WAS CHANGING SHAPE.
TAKE HERE, AS ONE INSTANCE. IN SINGAPORE, WHERE RA'S ONCE OPERATED A COMBINE THAT SHIPPED OPIUM AND HEROIN TO THREE QUARTERS OF THE WORLD.
OVER A PERIOD OF YEARS I REDIRECTED THE PURPOSE AND THE FLOW, SO THAT NOW THE SAME ORGANIZATION BRINGS FOOD AND MEDICINE TO MILLIONS!

I'D--SEEN SOME INDICATION OF THAT. I THOUGHT--I ASSUMED IT WAS JUST A FRONT!
SO DID--SO DO THE PEOPLE WHO WORKED FOR RA'S, AND NOW FOR ME.
WHAT THEY DID NOT NOTICE, BECAUSE IT HAPPENED SO SLOWLY, WAS THAT THE "FRONT" HAD BECOME THE ENTIRE OPERATION.

AND IT IS THAT OPERATION OVER WHICH I NOW WANT YOU TO ASSUME CONTROL, SON.
I HAVE SET THE MACHINERY IN MOTION --NOW SOMEONE ELSE MUST CONTINUE THE WORK.
BUT-- WHY...? IF YOU HAVE ACCOMPLISHED SO MUCH --WHY GIVE IT UP, EVEN TO ME?
FOR THE SIMPLEST REASON IMAGINABLE, SON.

"I WANT TO BE BATMAN AGAIN!"
THIS IS WHAT I'VE BEEN MISSING!

THE WIND IN MY FACE...
THE TUG OF MY CAPE ON MY SHOULDERS.

THE WAY THE MUSCLES OF MY ARMS SCREAM WHEN I PUSH THEM TO THEIR ABSOLUTE LIMITS!

IN THE LAST TWENTY YEARS, I'VE ACCOMPLISHED MORE ON A GLOBAL BASIS THAN I EVER COULD HAVE AS BATMAN...
POLICE

...BUT NOW, WITH BRUCE JR. AT THE HELM OF MY WORLDWIDE OPERATIONS...

...I CAN GET BACK TO THE JOB THAT REALLY GIVES MY LIFE ITS PURPOSE!
DON'T MESS WITH ME, MAN!
JUST HAND OVER THE CASE!

WHAT IF HE DOESN'T WANT TO?
HUH?

UNFH!!
B-BATMAN..?

IT--IT IS YOU!
BUT--I HEARD YOU'D LEFT GOTHAM! THERE WERE RUMORS--AFTER SUPERMAN WAS SENT INTO THE PHANTOM ZONE...
I... DID LEAVE GOTHAM, FOR A WHILE, FRIEND.

BUT YOU CAN BE THE FIRST TO TELL EVERYONE--
THE BATMAN IS BACK ON THE BEAT!
TAXI
AND HIS COMMENT HAS REMINDED ME OF ANOTHER TASK I NEED TO PERFORM.

IT'S NOT EXACTLY TEN YEARS...

...BUT I DON'T THINK ANYONE WILL BEGRUDGE A LITTLE TIME OFF FOR GOOD BEHAVIOR.

NO ONE HAS TOUCHED THE CONTROLS SINCE JUNIOR LOCKED THIS THING AWAY IN THAT SAFE.
ALL I HAVE TO DO IS PRESS THE SECOND BUTTON...

AND SUPERMAN WILL BE BACK AMONG THE LIVING!
BATMAN..!
YOU'VE CHANGED YOUR UNIFORM SINCE THE LAST TIME I SAW YOU!

MORE THAN THAT, OLD FRIEND. WELCOME HOME.
BRUCE! IS THAT REALLY YOU? I THOUGHT YOU WERE DEAD!
WE ALL DID!
AH...! AND YOU MUST BE KNIGHTWING!
IT'S A GREAT HONOR TO MEET YOU AT LAST, GRANDFATHER.
YES. MY FATHER CONTACTED ME, TO TELL ME YOU WERE COMING.
TO MEET BOTH OF YOU!
YOU'VE TURNED OUT TO BE A FINE YOUNG MAN, CLARK. I'VE WATCHED YOU GROW, WATCHED YOU WORK WITH BATMAN, FIRST AS ROBIN, THEN ON YOUR OWN AS KNIGHTWING.
YOU ARE A FINE HEIR TO THE HOUSE OF EL!
ER... CLARK...
"...HOUSE OF EL..."??

HE DOESN'T KNOW HE'S YOUR GRANDSON, REMEMBER?
HE THINKS MY SON IS HIS BIOLOGICAL FATHER!
THAT DECEPTION IS NO LONGER NECESSARY, BRUCE.
"TAKE ME TO LEX LUTHOR'S LAIR, AND I'LL SHOW YOU WHY!"
AS YOU CAN SEE, WE TOOK SOME PRECAUTIONS WITH THE TOWER, AFTER YOU WERE BANISHED INTO THE PHANTOM ZONE, SUPERMAN.
GREEN LANTERN SEALED THE WHOLE TOWER IN HIS MYSTICAL ENERGY, LIKE A DRAGONFLY CAUGHT IN AMBER!
THAT HASN'T DETERRED PEOPLE FROM TRYING TO GET INSIDE, TO STEAL LUTHOR'S SECRETS.
ALL OF THEM FAILED, BUT LANTERN AND I DECIDED TO LEAVE EVIDENCE OF THEIR ATTEMPTS, TO SHOW OTHERS HOW FUTILE IT WAS.
HOW DO WE GET IN?

EASY AS PIE, BATMAN.
ANYONE CARE TO TELL ME WHY, THOUGH?

I HAD TEN YEARS TO DO VERY LITTLE OTHER THAN THINK WHILE I WAS IN THE PHANTOM ZONE.
AND THERE WAS ONE THING THAT KEPT COMING BACK TO MY MIND. THE ULTRA-HUMANITE HAD TRANSPLANTED HIS BRAIN INTO LUTHOR'S SKULL...
...AND HE SAID HE INTENDED TO USE SOME KIND OF MIND-SWITCHING DEVICE TO TAKE OVER MY BODY.

BUT HE ALSO USED GOLD KRYPTONITE TO REMOVE MY POWERS--PERMANENTLY!
YET TWICE ULTRA SPOKE NOT ONLY OF HAVING MY BODY, BUT ALSO MY POWER. WAS HE SPEAKING METAPHORICALLY, OR...?
...OR DID HE HAVE A CURE FOR THE EFFECTS OF GOLD K!?
WE NEED TO SEARCH THIS PLACE TOP TO BOTTOM!
I'M THE BEST MAN FOR THAT LITTLE JOB!
I CAN RENDER THE TOWER INVISIBLE IN LAYERS! KEEP AN EYE OUT FOR ANYTHING THAT LOOKS LIKE WHAT WE WANT!
THERE!
YEP--MY RING SEEMS TO AGREE WITH YOU, K.W.!
THAT VIAL RESONATES AT THE SAME FREQUENCY AS KRYPTONITE.
NOT MUCH OF IT THERE.
EVEN ASSUMING WE'RE RIGHT-- HOW DO WE JUDGE THE "DOSAGE"?
ONLY ONE WAY...
SUPER-MAN!!

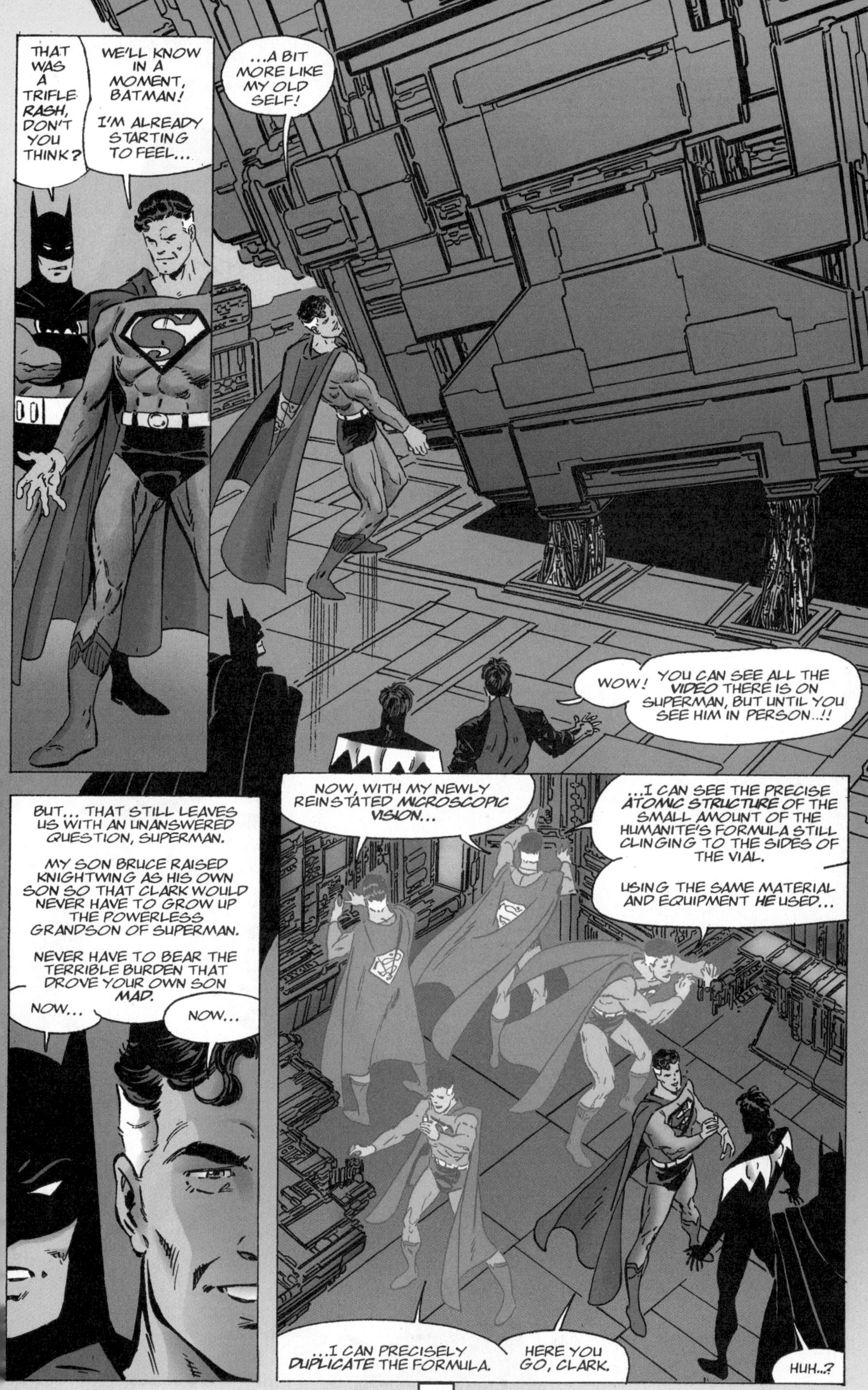
THAT WAS A TRIFLE RASH, DON'T YOU THINK?
WE'LL KNOW IN A MOMENT, BATMAN!
I'M ALREADY STARTING TO FEEL...
...A BIT MORE LIKE MY OLD SELF!
WOW!
YOU CAN SEE ALL THE VIDEO THERE IS ON SUPERMAN, BUT UNTIL YOU SEE HIM IN PERSON...!!
BUT... THAT STILL LEAVES US WITH AN UNANSWERED QUESTION, SUPERMAN.
MY SON BRUCE RAISED KNIGHTWING AS HIS OWN SON SO THAT CLARK WOULD NEVER HAVE TO GROW UP THE POWERLESS GRANDSON OF SUPERMAN.
NEVER HAVE TO BEAR THE TERRIBLE BURDEN THAT DROVE YOUR OWN SON MAD.
NOW...
NOW...
NOW, WITH MY NEWLY REINSTATED MICROSCOPIC VISION...
...I CAN SEE THE PRECISE ATOMIC STRUCTURE OF THE SMALL AMOUNT OF THE HUMANITE'S FORMULA STILL CLINGING TO THE SIDES OF THE VIAL.
USING THE SAME MATERIAL AND EQUIPMENT HE USED...
...I CAN PRECISELY DUPLICATE THE FORMULA.
HERE YOU GO, CLARK.
HUH...?

YOU DON'T MEAN TO TELL ME...
...ALL I HAVE TO DO IS DRINK THIS STUFF, AND I'LL HAVE THE SAME POWERS AS YOU, SUPERMAN...??
ON A REDUCED SCALE. YOUR KRYPTONIAN BLOOD HAS BEEN DILUTED BY TWO GENERATIONS OF INTERMARRIAGE WITH HUMANS.
BUT STILL ENOUGH TO BE IMPRESSIVE, I SHOULD THINK!
WOW!! I... I NEED TO THINK ABOUT THIS! IT'S ENOUGH FOR ONE DAY TO FIND OUT I'M REALLY SUPERMAN'S GRANDSON!
TO BE TOLD I CAN ALSO NOW INHERIT HIS POWERS...! THAT'S THE SORT OF THING THAT CHANGES A GUY'S LIFE A BIT!
THERE'S NO RUSH, CLARK! NOW THAT SUPERMAN HIMSELF IS BACK IN FORM, YOU CAN TAKE ALL THE TIME YOU NEED FOR YOUR DECISION!
WELL-- NOT QUITE.
"THERE'S ONE MORE THING I NEED TO TELL YOU ALL..."
YOU REALLY MEAN TO GO THROUGH WITH THIS?
YES. IN MY TEN YEARS IN THE PHANTOM ZONE I REALIZED IT'S REALLY THE ONLY THING I CAN DO.
ESPECIALLY NOW THAT THERE ARE SO MANY TO TAKE MY PLACE.
NO ONE CAN EVER DO THAT, GRANDFATHER!
YOU'RE GETTING PRETTY GOOD WITH THE FLYING, CLARK!
HARD TO BELIEVE YOU'VE ONLY HAD THOSE POWERS FOR A MONTH!
IT... SEEMS TO COME NATURALLY, BRUCE!
BUT... I HAVE TO SECOND BRUCE'S QUESTION, GRANDFATHER.

DO YOU REALLY HAVE TO LEAVE?
YES, CLARK. THE TIME HAS FINALLY COME, I THINK, FOR ME TO GO OUT INTO THE GALAXY, INTO THE UNIVERSE.
THERE ARE THINGS OUT THERE THAT ONLY SUPERMAN CAN TAKE CARE OF. WITH THE LIKES OF YOU, AND DIANA, AND KYLE, RICK, JANET AND BRUCE HERE TO TAKE CARE OF HER...
"...THE WORLD WILL BE IN THE BEST HANDS IT CAN BE!"
CAN YOU STILL SEE HIM?
YES. BUT HE'S RIGHT AT THE LIMIT OF MY TELESCOPIC VISION. MUST BE A HUNDRED LIGHT-YEARS AWAY, ALREADY.
RACK THIS UP AS ONE OF THE STRANGEST MONTHS OF MY LIFE, I GUESS!
I MEET MY GRANDFATHER, DISCOVER HE'S NOT REALLY MY GRANDFATHER, DISCOVER MY REAL GRANDFATHER IS SUPERMAN...
...AND THEN SEE SUPERMAN LEAVE EARTH--FOREVER!
OH, NOT "FOREVER," I'LL BET.
HE'LL BE BACK, FROM TIME TO TIME. JUST TO KEEP AN EYE ON ALL OF US.

"AFTER ALL--IF HE DID ANY LESS, HE WOULDN'T REALLY BE SUPERMAN!"

2919
Nineteen Twenty Nine

HE'S DEFINITELY ON THIS PLANET.
A NATURAL CHOICE--BLEAK, INHOSPITABLE, AND AS FAR FROM CIVILIZATION AS HE CAN POSSIBLY BE.
NOT UNLIKE HIS OLD FORTRESS OF SOLITUDE BACK ON EARTH!
MY FIELD-SUIT SHOULD BE ABLE TO HOLD OFF THE WORST THE PLANET'S ENVIRONMENT CAN THROW AT ME.
BUT EVEN THOUGH I'VE SET MYSELF DOWN RIGHT ON TOP OF THE SENSOR SIGNAL...
...I DON'T SEE ANYTHING THAT LOOKS LIKE A DOOR...
AH... APPARENTLY, MY ARRIVAL HAS BEEN DETECTED!

WHOA! THIS IS BIGGER THAN THE BATCAVE EVER WAS!
I GUESS HE'S COLLECTED A LOT OF SOUVENIRS IN A THOUSAND YEARS!
IT IS YOU!
I WAS HALFWAY CONVINCED MY PERIMETER SENSORS MUST BE GIVING ME A FALSE READING!
KAL! FINALLY SHOWING YOUR AGE, I SEE!
AND YOU! A FEW MORE WHITE HAIRS SINCE THE LAST TIME WE SAW EACH OTHER, BRUCE!
IS RA'S AL GHUL'S LAZARUS PIT WEARING OFF?
NO -- BUT I AM AGING ABOUT ONE YEAR FOR EVERY CENTURY!
HOW ABOUT YOU?

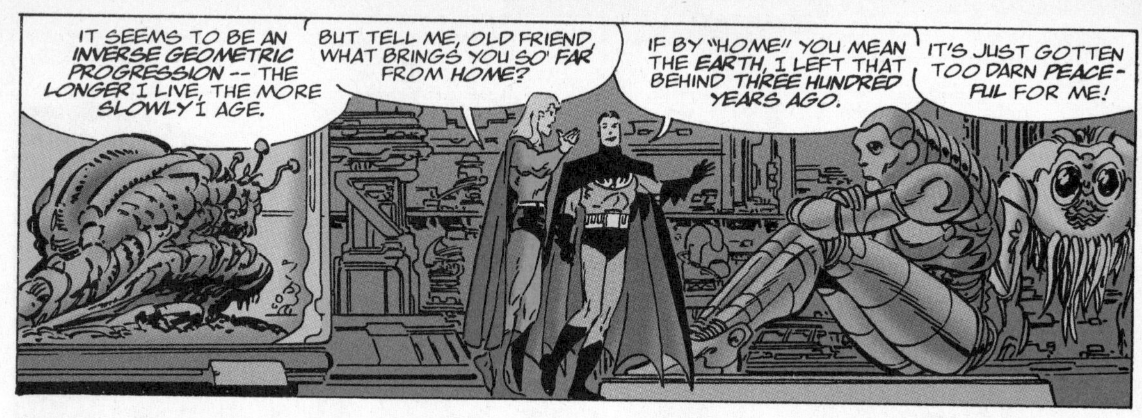

YES--AND IT'S ALMOST PROVIDENTIAL THAT YOU SHOULD SHOW UP JUST NOW.

I STILL COMMEMORATE THE TERRAN NEW YEAR, AND LAST MONTH, WHEN THE DATE TURNED TO 2919, IT GOT ME TO THINKING ABOUT WHEN YOU AND I FIRST MET.

BACK IN 1939, YOU MEAN? AT THE METROPOLIS WORLD'S FAIR?

I DON'T SEE HOW 2919 WOULD MAKE YOU THINK OF THAT, OUTSIDE OF GENERAL NOSTALGIA!

OH, IT WASN'T THAT MEETING I WAS REMEMBERING, BRUCE.

THAT WAS REALLY OUR SECOND MEETING.

"I WAS THINKING OF SOME-THING THAT HAPPENED TEN YEARS EARLIER..."
GOTHAM CITY!
SURE IS A LOT DIFFERENT FROM SMALLVILLE!
IF I'M REALLY GOING TO MOVE HERE WHEN I GRADUATE FROM JOURNALISM SCHOOL, I'D BETTER START MEMORIZING THE LAYOUT RIGHT NOW!

STARTING WITH THE LOCATION OF THE GOTHAM GAZETTE BUILDING!
AND THERE IT IS! SURE STANDS OUT, WITH ITS SUPER-MODERN ARCHITECTURE!
GAZETTE
I'M JUST IN TIME FOR MY APPOINTMENT WITH THE EDITOR IN CHIEF.
CLARK KENT'S APPOINTMENT, THAT IS!
OH, YES, MR. KENT--HE'S EXPECTING YOU. GO RIGHT ON IN.
THE OTHER WINNERS ARE ALREADY HERE.
THANKS!
AH, YOU MUST BE KENT, EH?
FIND YOUR WAY FROM THE TRAIN STATION OKAY, DID YOU?
YES, THANKS, MR. WHITNEY.
SAY HELLO TO YOUR FELLOW WINNERS, KENT.
BOBBY SHAW, RALPH WINGET, STAN COULTER...

...AND OUR ONLY FEMALE WINNER, MISS LOIS LANE.
HIYA.
≥GULP≤
NOW--EACH OF YOU IS HERE BECAUSE YOU CAME OUT AT THE TOP OF YOUR CLASSES AT YOUR VARIOUS JOURNALISM COLLEGES...
...AND WON THE GAZETTE'S ESSAY CONTEST. NOW IT'S TIME FOR YOU ALL TO MEET THE YOUNG MAN WHO MADE THIS POSSIBLE...
...MR. BRUCE WAYNE.
THANK YOU, MR. WHITNEY.
AND THANK ALL OF YOU FOR COMING.

GLAD TO BE HERE, WAYNE.

BUT MAYBE YOU'D CARE TO TELL US WHY A KID WHO COMES UP NUMBER *FIFTEEN* ON THE *COUNTRY'S RICHEST MEN LIST* WANTS TO SPEND HIS MONEY SPONSORING JOURNALISM COMPETITIONS?

I'D BE HAPPY TO, MISS LANE.

NINE YEARS AGO, MY PARENTS, THOMAS AND MARTHA WAYNE, WERE BRUTALLY GUNNED DOWN BEFORE MY EYES AS WE WERE WALKING HOME FROM A DOUGLAS FAIRBANKS PICTURE.

I INHERITED MY FATHER'S FORTUNE, AND IN THE TIME SINCE I HAVE ALMOST *DOUBLED* ITS VALUE.

MUCH OF THAT WEALTH I HAVE USED TO CREATE CHARITIES WHICH FIGHT *POVERTY* AND *IGNORANCE* IN GOTHAM CITY...

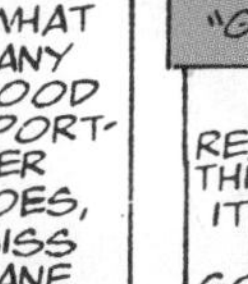

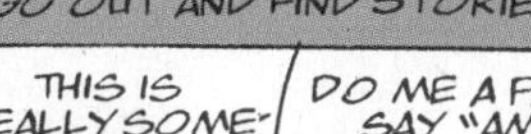

IS THAT WHERE YOU'RE FROM, LOIS? MR. WHITNEY DIDN'T SAY.
NO--I'M FROM EVERYWHERE. MY DAD'S IN THE ARMY. BUT METROPOLIS IS WHERE I'M HEADING.
I ONLY CAME ON THIS CORNY JUNKET SO I COULD GET SOME PRINT THAT WOULD IMPRESS THE E-I-C OF THE DAILY PLANET...!!
IS THAT WHERE YOU'RE PLANNING TO...
HOLY COW! LOOK!
GOTH

LOIS! LOOK OUT!
WE DON'T HAVE TO LOOK ANY FURTHER FOR A STORY, KENT!
IT'S COME TO US!
THERE'S SOMEONE DRIVING THAT THING! WHO..?
OMIGOSH! IT'S LEX!!
YOU'VE GOT TO GET OUT OF HARM'S WAY, LOIS!
STAY HERE IN THIS DOORWAY!
I'M GOING TO FIND HELP!

THE LAST TIME I SAW LEX HE WAS BOUND FOR THE SMALLVILLE JUVENILE DETENTION HOME.
HE MUST HAVE ESCAPED AND FOUND HIS WAY TO GOTHAM.
BUT--WHERE DID HE FIND THAT ROBOT?
OH, NO!
IT'S GOT LOIS! SHE DIDN'T STAY IN HIDING!
LET GO OF ME, YOU BIG LUMMOX!!
YOU HEARD THE LADY, LUTHOR!
PUT HER DOWN--GENTLY!
SUPERBOY!!
I WAS ALMOST HOPING YOU WOULD TURN UP!
UNGH!
"THIS IS THE OPPORTUNITY I'VE BEEN WAITING FOR!

A PERFECT CHANCE TO TEST SOME OF THESE SKILLS I'VE BEEN HONING.
ALFRED--BRING IT.
AS YOU WISH, MASTER BRUCE.

ARE YOU QUITE CERTAIN YOU WISH TO DO THIS, MASTER BRUCE?
MORE CERTAIN THAN I HAVE BEEN OF ANYTHING IN MY LIFE, ALFRED.

I'VE BEEN PREPARING MYSELF FOR THIS EVERY DAY SINCE MY PARENTS WERE MURDERED.

NOW IT'S TIME TO PUT THAT PREPARATION TO GOOD USE!

I'LL HAVE TO SECOND SUPERBOY'S REQUEST, WHOEVER YOU ARE IN THERE.
LET THE GIRL GO!
ANOTHER ONE!
BUT WITHOUT ANY POWERS THIS TIME!
I CAN SWAT YOU AWAY AS EASILY AS I DID SUPERBOY!
DON'T COUNT ON IT, FRIEND!
I'VE ALREADY CALCULATED THE ARC OF THE ARMS, AND THEY CAN'T TOUCH ME HERE!
AND THIS SHAPED CHARGE CAN OPEN YOUR COCKPIT AS EASY AS A CAN OF SARDINES!
BLAST!
MY CALCULATIONS DID NOT INCLUDE DEALING WITH A PAIR OF COSTUMED INTERLOPERS.
I BELIEVE I SHALL PRACTICE THE BETTER PART OF VALOR!
HEY!

NOT SO FAST, LEX!
YOU MAY HAVE KNOCKED THE WIND OUT OF ME WITH THAT THERMAL BLAST...
...BUT I'M READY FOR YOU NOW!
ARE YOU, SUPERBOY?
TAKE A LOOK BEHIND YOU!
OH, NO!
THE ROBOT IS RUNNING AMOK!
CATCH ME OR STOP THE ROBOT, SUPERBOY!
EVEN YOU CAN'T DO BOTH!
HE'S RIGHT, BLAST HIM!
I'VE GOT TO STOP THAT THING BEFORE SOMEONE IS KILLED!
ESPECIALLY SINCE THAT "SOMEONE" MIGHT BE LOIS LANE!
CRUNCH

YOU'LL BE SAFE OVER HERE, MISS.
NOW TO GET YOUR RED-BREASTED FRIEND OUT OF TROUBLE!
SUPERBOY! HE DID SOMETHING TO FUSE THE CONTROLS! NOTHING WORKS!
JUMP CLEAR! I'M GOING TO TAKE THE DIRECT APPROACH TO HANDLING THIS THING!
ALL YOURS, SUPERBOY!

AND THE FAR SIDE OF THE MOON SEEMS LIKE AN IDEAL LOCATION!
IF WE CAN'T CONTROL THIS THING, OR TURN IT OFF...
...MY BEST BET IS TO PLACE IT SOMEWHERE THAT IT CAN'T DO ANY HARM!
"NOW TO GET BACK TO GOTHAM AND FIND OUT WHO OUR MASKED FRIEND IS!"
THERE YOU GO, MISS. YOU SHOULD BE ABLE TO SLIP OUT OF THE CLAW'S GRIP, NOW.
THANKS, ROBIN RED-BREAST.
BUT WHO ARE YOU, AND WHERE DID YOU COME FROM?
JUST THE QUESTION I WAS GOING TO ASK.
I'D PREFER TO KEEP MY TRUE IDENTITY SECRET, SUPERBOY, JUST AS YOU DO.
HOWEVER, I THINK THIS YOUNG LADY'S "SUGGESTION" WILL WORK FOR NOW. CALL ME ROBIN!
HUH! BIT SISSY FOR A GROWNUP, DON'T YOU THINK? KINDA LIKE OUR FLYING HE-MAN HERE CALLING HIMSELF SUPERBOY.
ER... WELL, I WAS THINKING IT MIGHT BE TIME TO CHANGE TO SUPERMAN, BUT...

YES, WELL, I'M SURE THAT KIND OF FASCINATING CONTEMPLATION FILLS JUST HOURS OF YOUR DAY, SUPERBOY.
ME, THOUGH, I WANT A LITTLE MORE ACTIVITY IN MY LIFE.
LIKE FINDING OUT WHERE THAT BIG ROBOT CAME FROM, FOR A START!
THAT BIG CRATE--OR WHAT'S LEFT OF IT--LOOKS LIKE A GOOD PLACE TO FIND CLUES.
YES--THERE ARE MICROSCOPIC DUST AND POLLEN PARTICLES MIXED IN WITH THE PACKING MATERIAL...
EXCELLENT, SUPERBOY! IF YOU CAN ISOLATE SOME OF THEM, I CAN TELL WITHIN A HUNDRED SQUARE MILES WHERE THEY ORIGINATED!
SOME-WHERE NEAR THE LAB OF ONE STANIS-LAUS ERWIN!
WHY WOULD YOU SAY THAT, MISS LANE?
KEEN DEDUCTIVE REASONING, ROBBIE. THAT...
...AND THE FACT THAT HIS NAME AND ADDRESS ARE ON THE SHIPPING LABEL...

THERE'S THE BUILDING THAT HOUSES ERWIN'S LAB. PRETTY SEEDY PART OF TOWN, EVEN FOR GOTHAM!
LOOK, THERE'S ROBIN'S MOTOR-CYCLE!
HE MUST KNOW GOTHAM LIKE THE BACK OF HIS HAND, TO HAVE BEATEN US HERE OVERLAND!
YOU, ER, SOUND PRETTY IMPRESSED WITH HIM, MISS LANE.
YEAH, WELL, I'M ALWAYS MORE IMPRESSED WITH BRAINS THAN BRAWN, SUPERBOY.
AH, THERE YOU ARE! THIS IS DR. ERWIN. HE'S BEEN TELLING ME QUITE A TALE!
YES--THIS YOUNG MAN YOU CALL LEX LUTHOR CAME TO ME LOOKING FOR A JOB AS A LAB ASSISTANT, AND CALLING HIMSELF REX THORUL.
"HE WORKED HARD, AND HIS SKILLS WERE QUITE EXCEPTIONAL FOR ONE HIS AGE...
"...BUT ONE DAY I CAME ACROSS SOME SCRAPS OF PAPER ON WHICH HE HAD DRAWN UP PLANS TO USE MY ROBOT TO ROB THE GOTHAM CENTRAL BANK.
WHAT IS THE MEANING OF THIS, REX?
YOU'RE JEALOUS OF ME! JUST LIKE EVERYONE ELSE!
JEALOUS OF MY GENIUS!

HE STORMED OUT, AND I THOUGHT I WOULD NEVER SEE HIM AGAIN.
THAT WAS A WEEK AGO, AND I WENT AHEAD WITH SHIPPING MY ROBOT TO GOTHAM AS PLANNED. I SUPPOSE I SHOULD HAVE KNOWN THORUL--OR LUTHOR WOULD NOT HAVE ABANDONED HIS PLANS, EITHER.
WELL, SUPERBOY, YOU KNOW THIS LUTHOR CHARACTER. DOES THAT SOUND LIKE HIM TO YOU?
VERY MUCH. I'D BELIEVE THIS STORY IMPLICITLY, ROBIN...
...IF MY SUPER-KEEN SENSE OF SMELL WASN'T DETECTING RECENTLY APPLIED SPIRIT GUM--AND ONE VERY LARGE RAT!
NO!
LUTHOR!
LOIS! LOOK OUT!
YOU AGAIN!
THIS IS TWICE YOU'VE BEEN IN THE WRONG PLACE AT THE WRONG TIME! THERE SHALL NOT BE A THIRD!
NOT SO FAST, LEX! THERE'S NOTHING TO DISTRACT ME, THIS TIME!

NO? HOW ABOUT THIS SMALL ROCK SAMPLE I RETRIEVED FROM MY LODGINGS?
UHNGH!!
KRYPTO-NITE!
LET GO OF ME!
LET GO OF ME!
AND SO IT ENDS AS WE ALWAYS KNEW IT WOULD, SUPERBOY!
THOUGH WE WERE ONCE FRIENDS, YOUR JEALOUSY COST ME MY GREATEST DISCOVERY, AND MY HAIR!
NOW, MY SUPERIOR INTELLECT WILL COST YOU YOUR LIFE!
MAYBE NOT JUST YET, LUTHOR!
IT'S A LONG SHOT, BUT IF I CAN BEND THIS STRIP OF METAL TO PRECISELY THE CORRECT CURVATURE...
...I CAN MAKE USE OF SOMETHING I LEARNED IN AUSTRALIA TWO YEARS AGO.
SAY "FAREWELL" TO THE WORLD, SUPERBOY! AND AS YOU DIE, THINK OF ALL THE PEOPLE WHO WILL NOW SUFFER AS I...
EH..??
OW!!

PERFECT! AND THIS **LEAD PIPE** WILL BLOCK THE KRYPTONITE RADIATION...

...WHILE I FINISH UP THE JOB WITH LUTHOR!

FINISH UP **THIS**, PRETTY BOY!

I'VE NO MORE TIME TO WASTE WITH THE LIKES OF YOU!

OH!

LOIS!

WITH MY **HELI-PACK** AT FULL POWER, I CAN BE MILES AWAY BEFORE...

GOING SOMEWHERE, LEX?

LOOKS LIKE FALL CAME A LITTLE EARLY THIS YEAR, EH, LEX?
≥GROAN≤
PLEASE, SUPERBOY --NO PUNS!
NICELY DONE, BLUE-BOY! I MAY HAVE TO RAISE MY ESTIMATION OF YOU A NOTCH OR TWO!
I DIDN'T REALIZE IT NEEDED RAISING, MISS LANE.
THE HARDEST, SUPERBOY. BUT YOU'VE DONE BETTER'N MOST TODAY!
SEEMS LIKE YOU'RE A HARD GIRL TO IMPRESS!
PLEASE--SPARE ME THE SWEET NOTHINGS! ANY JAIL WOULD BE PREFERABLE!
THE POLICE ARE ON THEIR WAY, LUTHOR
"YOU'LL BE BACK WHERE YOU BELONG, SOON ENOUGH!"
IT MAKES ME SAD, EVERY TIME I SEE LEX HAULED OFF TO PRISON AGAIN. SUCH A GREAT MIND, GONE BAD!
SAVE YOUR COMPASSION FOR THE PEOPLE WHO DESERVE IT, SUPERBOY! ONCE A MAN STRAYS FROM THE STRAIGHT AND NARROW, HE GETS NO SYMPATHY FROM ME!
WELL! AND HOW DID YOU GET TO BE SUCH A HARD-HEARTED LITTLE BIRDIE?
POLICE
WE'RE ALL DONE HERE, SUPERBOY. ANY OF YOU KIDS NEED A RIDE SOMEWHERE?
THAT WOULD BE ME, I GUESS. THE BOYS HAVE THEIR OWN MEANS OF TRANSPORTATION.
BUT BEFORE I GO...

HERE'S A LITTLE SOMETHING TO REMEMBER ME BY!
"SO YOU WON'T BE MOVING TO GOTHAM CITY AFTER ALL, SON?"
NO, PA! I'VE DECIDED THERE ARE... MORE OPPORTUNITIES FOR ME IN METROPOLIS, AT THE DAILY PLANET.
CLARK! CLARK, COME QUICK!
PETE ROSS! LAND O' GOSHEN, YOUNGSTER, WHATEVER IS THE MATTER?
IT'S LANA! SHE WAS FOOLING AROUND WITH A MAGIC WAND HER FATHER BROUGHT BACK FROM MERLIN'S CAVE...
"...AND IT'S TRANSFORMED HER INTO SOME KIND OF SORCERESS!"
OH, BROTHER! HERE WE GO AGAIN!
SUPERBOY! I WAS HOPING YOU'D SHOW UP!
COME! TOGETHER WE CAN PUT RIGHT ALL THE ILLS OF THE WORLD!
"SO YOU KNEW I WAS THE FIRST 'ROBIN' ALL ALONG?"

NOT AT THAT TIME--BUT AFTER I LEARNED BRUCE WAYNE WAS THE BATMAN, AND A WHILE LATER BATMAN TURNED UP WITH A PARTNER CALLED "ROBIN"...
YES... YOU WERE NOT THE ONLY ONE TO MAKE THAT CONNECTION, OLD FRIEND!

STILL--REMINISCING ABOUT OLD TIMES IS NOT WHY I SPENT THE LAST TWO YEARS TRACKING YOU DOWN.
I HAD THE FUTURE IN MIND, NOT THE PAST.
WHAT DO YOU MEAN, BRUCE?

I MEAN--WE'RE THE LAST ONES, KAL. EVERYONE ELSE IS DEAD NOW. WE'RE THE LAST ONES WHO REMEMBER HOW IT WAS WHEN WE STARTED.
HOW IT WAS WHEN EVERYTHING WAS ROUGH AND TUMBLE, AND WE MADE OUR OWN RULES.
WHEN THE WORLD WAS CRYING OUT FOR PEACE AND ORDER, AND WE WERE THE ONES WHO FOUND THE WAYS TO PROVIDE IT!
A LITTLE TOO SUCCESSFULLY, AS IT TURNED OUT!

EXACTLY! YOU, ME, OUR FRIENDS AND OFFSPRING--WE MADE THE WORLD A BETTER PLACE, NEARLY A PERFECT PLACE. AND IN THE PROCESS, WE MADE OURSELVES REDUNDANT.
AND FOR US, LOSING PURPOSE IS LIKE LOSING OUR SOUL.
WHICH IS WHY I WITHDREW FURTHER AND FURTHER FROM A GALAXY THAT SEEMED TO HAVE NO MORE USE FOR THE LIKES OF ME.

SO LET'S DO SOMETHING ABOUT IT, KAL!
THE UNIVERSE IS A BIG PLACE! THERE MUST BE WORLDS, SYSTEMS, MAYBE WHOLE GALAXIES OUT THERE THAT STILL NEED A COUPLE OF OLD WAR HORSES LIKE US!
WHAT DO YOU..?
HELLO, MR. WAYNE. IT'S BEEN A LONG TIME.
YOU...MAKE AN INTRIGUING ARGUMENT, BRUCE.
ONLY--IT JUST WOULDN'T BE THE TWO OF US...
LANA..?? LANA LANG ??
YOU TWO AREN'T THE ONLY IMMORTALS AROUND HERE. ALL THOSE POTIONS AND SPELLS AND FORMULAS I MESSED WITH OVER THE YEARS HAD A PERMANENT EFFECT.
THREE HUNDRED YEARS AGO, LANA TRACKED ME DOWN, AS YOU DID, BRUCE.
AND THE TWO OF YOU ARE..?
WELL--I MUST SAY, I APPROVE! I LOVED LOIS LIKE A SISTER, BUT YOU TWO HAD SO MUCH HISTORY...!
AND EVEN AFTER KAL LEFT SMALLVILLE, I NEVER REALLY STOPPED LOVING HIM.
SHE WAITED SEVEN HUNDRED YEARS FOR ME, BRUCE. THERE NEVER WAS A GREATER TESTIMONY TO TRUE LOVE!

BUT, HEY, ENOUGH TALK! WE CAN ALL GET CAUGHT UP LATER!
LIKE BRUCE SAID, IT'S A BIG UNIVERSE--THERE MUST BE SOMEWHERE OUT THERE THE THREE OF US CAN GET INTO TROUBLE!
NEVER THE END